UNITY IN DIVERSITY

THE WAY AHEAD FOR HUMANITY

BENJAMIN CREME

Share International Foundation
Amsterdam • London

Manufactured in the United States on recycled paper

First Edition, June 2012

*The painting by Benjamin Creme reproduced on the cover is entitled **Mandala – Unity in Diversity** (c.1969).*

This book is dedicated to my revered Master
without Whose vision and wisdom
it could not have been written.

TABLE OF CONTENTS

PREFACE

In this coming time, as we move deeper into the Aquarian experience, we will find that the idea of unity and its relation to diversity becomes ever more meaningful, and consistent with our growing understanding of the evolution of consciousness, which is the central purpose of our human existence. Unity to the Masters is the inner reality of our lives, reflecting the unity of every atom in relation with every other atom in cosmos. We all seek unity, knowingly or not: it is the destined achievement of our longing and our creating. Our aspiration for betterment drives us towards unity. Diversity also, we shall understand, is the reality of our being, reflecting as it does each person's unique individuality. We have to realise that humanity is One, and act accordingly.

In this book I attempt to show some of the profound and far-reaching happenings that underlie the path to unity; also the parts that particular nations, in all their diversity, are playing in furthering the Plan of evolution, as understood and initiated by the Spiritual Hierarchy of Masters in this world cycle. The book comprises ten articles by one of the Masters of Wisdom, interspersed with talks by myself, and related questions and answers. Topics range from the political and international to group relationships, all with the underlying esoteric theme of unity in diversity, along with commentaries on related current affairs in the first decade of the 21st century.

Humanity's diversity is to a large extent the result of the differences in individual and national ray structures. The Rays are streams of energy, seven in number, which each person and each nation displays as part of their energetic make-up. The different ray qualities are expressed on the soul and the personality level for both individuals and nations. They qualify and give colour to the quality of the individual and nation. A few older nations display something of their soul quality but most, above all young nations, display mainly their personality ray. The same is true of the individual. This being so, the quality and identity of a nation is created mainly by the more advanced individuals in any country.

A great threefold experiment is being undertaken in the building of national identities: different ways of creating a unity from diversity. In the United Kingdom representatives of all the peoples of the Commonwealth of nations live together more or less peacefully, while strongly maintaining their separate identities. The USA is really an amalgam of representatives of many European countries transplanted across the ocean, mixing together until something new emerges – an American. The now independent states of the old USSR maintain their independence, while remaining a part of a vast 'federation', spreading from Europe to Vladivostok.

It will be seen that three great ideologies – democracy, communism and fascism – that today have divided humanity are actually our attempts to express, however inadequately and with much distortion, our vague awareness of the three aspects of the divine intention that we can know at this time. This shows the need for greater tolerance for different political structures. In the same way, working groups need to find ways to integrate the different individuals that make up those groups, and to work towards consensus and unity. Unity is the only path forward for all of humanity.

Background information

These lectures and answers to questions were addressed primarily to groups familiar with my information and previous publications. Therefore I speak freely about the Lord Maitreya and the Masters of Wisdom, without the need to explain Who They are, Their work and relation to humanity. For new readers, however, some explanation is essential and I offer the following brief account of Their work and plans.

The Masters of Wisdom are a group of perfected men Who have preceded us in evolution and indeed have reached a point where They need no further incarnation on our planet. Nevertheless, They remain on Earth to oversee the evolution of the rest of us. They are the Custodians of the evolutionary process, the Guides, the Mentors, the Protectors of the race, and work to fulfil the Plan of evolution of our Planetary Logos through humanity and the lower kingdoms. For many thousands of years They (and Their predecessors) have lived mainly in the remote mountain and desert areas of the world – the Himalaya, Andes, Rockies, Cascades, Carpathians, Atlas, Urals, and the Gobi and other deserts. From these mountain and desert retreats They have overseen and stimulated human evolution from behind the scenes.

For over 500 years They have prepared Themselves for a group return to the everyday world which, I submit, is now in progress. In July 1977, Their head and leader, the Lord Maitreya, Who embodies the Christ Principle (the energy of Love) and holds the office of World Teacher, descended from His Himalayan retreat and entered London, England, His 'point of focus' in the modern world. Maitreya lives in the Asian community of London as an 'ordinary' man awaiting the appropriate time to come openly before the world. He is expected by religious groups under different names: the Christ; the Imam Mahdi; the Messiah; Krishna; Maitreya Buddha. He does not come as a religious leader but as an educator in the broadest sense.

Maitreya's presence will galvanise humanity into making the necessary changes in our political, economic and social life that will guarantee peace, justice and freedom for all humanity. His major concern is the disparity in living standards between the developed and developing worlds, which, He says, threatens the future of the race. Terrorism is one of the main symptoms of these divisions. Maitreya sees the principle of sharing as the key to the solution of our manifold problems, and the means of bringing humanity into right relationship. Maitreya has said: "Take your brother's need as the measure for your action and solve the problems of the world. There is no other course." Since January 2010 Maitreya has appeared on television (still incognito) in America, Mexico and Brazil, and will continue to give interviews in Japan, Europe and many countries around the world.

In January 1959 I was contacted by one of the Masters in the Himalaya and soon after by Maitreya, Himself. I was offered the task of preparing the way for Their emergence, creating the climate of hope and expectancy, a task on which I have been engaged now for 38 years. In the course of the training by my Master to prepare me for this work, we have established a moment-to-moment two-way telepathic link. This enables Him to communicate with me, with the minimum of His attention and energy. He forged an instrument through whom He could work, and which would be responsive to His slightest impression (of course, with my complete co-operation and without the slightest infringement of my free will). The Master's articles contained in this book were dictated by Him originally for *Share International* magazine.

Further information about Maitreya and the Masters can be found in my books, as well as in *Share International* magazine and on the *Share International* website, details of which are given at the end of this book.

I wish to acknowledge my indebtedness to groups of people in London and the USA whose work have made possible the publication of this book. My particular thanks go to Michiko Ishikawa, from Berkeley, California, who has again organised and brought into readable form the diverse material of the book's content.

London, March 2012
Benjamin Creme

Editor's note: Benjamin Creme's talk on unity in diversity, and related questions and answers in this book, were given to groups in the USA associated with the author. It follows therefore that many of the questions are from an American perspective and from a particularly contentious period in that country's history.

The rest of the questions and answers were originally published in *Share International* magazine between 2006 and 2011, and, with a few exceptions, have not been published in previous books. The date of original publication is given at the end of each question.

UNITY IN DIVERSITY

MAITREYA'S PRIORITIES

by the Master —, through Benjamin Creme

While the world waits, expectantly, for Maitreya, and deliverance, there still remains much to do to secure the planet and mankind. Nevertheless, men have little time to wait for Maitreya to begin His open service. Short, indeed, therefore, is the time left to prepare His way, to tell men that help and hope are at hand, that the Teacher is here, eager to speak directly to the peoples of all the nations.

Speed, then, your efforts. Make haste to inform all who will listen that the destined hour has arrived, that soon mankind will rejoice in the presence of the Teacher. Tell them this and uphold their hope and courage. Many will listen now who before did not; anxiety and fear have taken their toll of men. The signs, too, have done their work and awakened millions to expected happenings and revelations. Never before in man's history have so many sensed the coming changes nor understood their necessity.

Hence, into an expectant and prepared world will Maitreya emerge, sure in the knowledge that His presence is longed for and eagerly anticipated.

Maitreya will outline for men the priorities which alone will secure and safeguard planet Earth and all its peoples. The necessity of peace is paramount for without peace all else is lost. Peace, He will affirm, can only be ensured through the creation of Justice. The lack of Justice is the begetter of both war and terrorism. Justice, Maitreya will maintain, can be achieved only through Sharing. Sharing, therefore, is the key to world peace and security.

Maitreya will turn the minds of men more urgently to the ills of planet Earth, itself. Without a healthy and robust planet the future of succeeding generations is in peril.

Maitreya will stress the urgency of action now to restore equilibrium to our suffering planetary home, and call all hands, old and young, to this primary task.

The fate of those who now starve in a world of plenty will exercise Maitreya's chief concern: "Nothing so moves Me to grief as this shame," He says, and seeks to galvanise the creation of a vast programme of aid for the world's poor on a scale hitherto unknown.

These are the immediate priorities, to make fast and secure the future for men. Man's free will is sacrosanct and may not be infringed; the speed of implementation of these primary requirements is subject, therefore, to the will of men.

Men now face the choice: to see the world as One and share, and know security and blessed Peace and happiness, or to witness the end of life on Earth.

Maitreya is emerging now to ensure that man's choice is wisely made. Have no fear, Maitreya already knows man's answer, and is glad.

(*Share International*, October 2006)

UNITY IN DIVERSITY

by the Master —, through Benjamin Creme

Throughout the centuries, men have adopted many different forms of government, ranging from the most despotic to the most egalitarian. Today, most countries have opted for a democratic form, that is, one elected by popular vote for one or other political party. It is assumed that the voting system used is fair, honest, free from malpractice and fraud.

Unfortunately, as recent history shows, this is often not the case, even in those countries which lay great stress on the probity of their election process. Deception and duplicity abound, men and factions are brought to power by chicanery and guile.

More authoritarian are those one-party states where decisions are made by a committee of 'strong men' backed by the army and police. The people have little say in the laws which rule them and often, as yet, do not feel the need to claim such rights.

Some countries are in the grip of cruel despots, hungry for power and the wealth which comes with it. Some are ruled by deluded zealots, sure that they and their followers are in the hands of God and are carrying out His plans. Others are struggling to help their people out of poverty and pain, and to fend off the demands of their wealthy neighbours.

Still others are fighting for their independence or are engulfed in chaos and civil war.

Men must take to heart the lesson from this evidence: many are the ways of organising the needs of different peoples. Greater tolerance, therefore, is necessary in the approach to this vital matter. The energies of the rays governing the nations are different and require different structures in which to express their qualities. It is not the Evolutionary Plan that one form of government, democratic or otherwise, should prevail. The needs of men are more real

15

and more important than ideologies. Tolerance of difference unites, while ideologies divide.

When Maitreya speaks openly, therefore, He will show that unity in diversity is the key to future harmony. That all the nations have a destiny, unique and sacred. He will point the way to achieving this blessed state and encourage men to open their hearts to a wiser understanding of the Plan. Under Maitreya's guidance, men will come to appreciate and value the richness of the achievements of themselves and others. The urge to compete and to dominate will gradually subside and a new chapter will open for men in brotherhood and peace. Thus will it be.

(Share International, May 2006)

COMMENTARY ON 'UNITY IN DIVERSITY'

The following article is an edited version of a talk given by Benjamin Creme at the Transmission Meditation Conference held near San Francisco, USA, in August 2006. Published in **Share International**, *January/February 2007.*

Before I talk about my views on the Master's article, 'Unity in Diversity' [reprinted in the previous pages] and try to expand on it, I would like to refresh your minds about the perennial needs of humanity, listed under the title of 'Maitreya's Priorities'.* I do this because if these are correct, and I believe that they are, these priorities, when held before our eyes and constantly engaging our attention, will be the more quickly fulfilled. Whatever our attention is withdrawn from will obviously not be fulfilled, and that is happening today.

Every few years there is a crisis – an earthquake, a tsunami, or a terrible famine engulfing parts of Africa or elsewhere. Immediately, the hearts of humanity are awakened to this crisis, and people pull out every stop to raise as much money as possible to meet the critical need of the time. While that crisis is given attention, that need is met. Enormous amounts of money are donated and directed to solving the needs of the stricken country. After a month or two the media stop asking for more money. The need seems to have been answered, whether the aid was correctly distributed or not. The thoughtform of need, of sudden, desperate urgency, disappears from our thinking and we go back to our own affairs.

How many fundraising concerts have we had? How many times have people raised money for charity, under the banner, 'Save the Starving Millions'? It is a 'one-off' happening every few years, whereas the starving millions of the world need real economic justice. Maitreya, you can be sure, will face humanity squarely with the continuing need to end the catastrophe that occurs every day: 35,000 people die of starvation in a world of plenty. Day after day, week after week, month after month, year after year that catastrophe goes on and on. It is time to face this tragic situation for millions of people and end it for ever.

I believe it will take Maitreya to do that – not Maitreya Himself, but the presence of Maitreya, the teachings of Maitreya, the urgency brought to bear by Maitreya, the shame, as He calls it. "Nothing so moves Me to grief as this shame," He says. "The crime of separation must be driven from this world. I affirm that as My purpose." That is the first purpose, the saving of the starving millions in the world. It is useful for groups of this kind to concentrate on and always keep before them the priorities of Maitreya, not just at a talk, but always to be aware of the major needs of humanity at large.

I will remind you once again of the priorities of Maitreya as seen by my Master, given in the article 'The Son of Man' (*Share International*, June 1984).

"Let us look at His priorities: the establishment of peace; the inauguration of the system of sharing; the removal of guilt and fear; the cleansing of the hearts and minds of men; the education of mankind in the Laws of Life and Love; an introduction to the Mysteries [the mysteries of initiation]*; the beautification of cities; the removal of barriers to travel and interchange of peoples; and the creation of a pool of knowledge accessible to all."*

That last one, "the pool of knowledge accessible to all", you might see as the internet when it is freely available to all, as it is not at the present time. When it is freely available to all, every country without exception, every people, nothing withheld that humanity needs, that will be like everyone owning all of the books in the libraries of Alexandria.

With that in mind, let us look again at the words of the Master in His article 'Unity in Diversity'.

"Throughout the centuries, men have adopted many different forms of government, ranging from the most despotic to the most egalitarian."

The most despotic we would hope to be in the past, and I think this is broadly so; the really big despots, the Genghis Khans and the like, are fortunately in the past, but there are still many despots around, some of very recent date. One could think of Hitler and Mussolini and company. One can think of the various right-wing, military dictatorships which this country, the United States, has foisted on South American countries like Chile.

Chile had a freely elected democratic government under Salvador Allende, which just happened to be left-wing. That was unacceptable to the government of the United States, so they got rid of him. The CIA created a coup, which overthrew Allende and his government, and installed a fascist-type dictator, a close friend of Mrs Thatcher, General Pinochet, well known for his despotic rule. When called before the courts for trial for his deeds, he always had a heart condition, could not walk, was too ill even to come to court to face his accusers.

"Today, most countries have opted for a democratic form, that is, one elected by popular vote for one or other political party. It is assumed that the voting system used is fair, free from malpractice and fraud."

If only that were true. One of the tragedies for the United States and for the world has been the extraordinary way in which the present administration [of President George W. Bush] was catapulted to power by the most fraudulent, corrupt malpractice in the entire history of malpractices, going back to 18th and 19th century England.

That was a time when would-be members of Parliament would buy votes by the gallon – gallons of beer that is. They would go through all the little towns and give everybody pints, as many as they could drink, and a hearty meal in the course of it, and gold coins that were worth a guinea apiece. These gold guineas put dozens of men into Parliament for no better reason than that they were businessmen, and being a member of Parliament would be good for their business. It gave them power and influence, which otherwise they would not have had. Malpractice was just the name of the game.

Nowadays elections in Britain are much fairer. They are not 100 per cent clean, but they are fairer. Usually, during an election or afterwards, it arises that, not the party as a whole, but the local party in some town, has worked out a scheme in which they can snaffle more than their share of the votes; that happens. In Britain, the 'mother of parliaments', small-time electoral fraud still goes on, but we have never seen anywhere in modern times the kind of corruption that was practised in the US election for President Bush's second term. We are all aware of the malpractice in the previous election that brought him to power in the first place. Al Gore won the first election and was denied it. Kerry won the second election decisively and was denied it.

I understand that one of the tricks played (only one of many) was that, in those areas of the country where electronic voting was used, one of the main suppliers of the voting machines was a key fundraiser for the Republican Party. His firm rigged the machines so that every fifth vote for Kerry was automatically turned into a vote for Bush. I know a woman in Massachusetts who used a machine for her vote. She voted for Kerry; the machine had an apparatus by which you could check that your vote had actually registered. She checked it and it came out Bush. She checked it again and it was Bush again. It gave Bush 18 times before it came up Kerry. You cannot imagine the scale of the fraud in the last US election. It has been for the world an absolute tragedy.

I cannot prove it of course, but I am convinced that if Al Gore had won the first election (which he did), 9/11 would not have taken place. I am sure it was planned before that. The planning would have gone on, but I think the actions of Gore would have been so different from those of the present administration that there would not have been the same sense of urgency and the same will to carry out 9/11.

If 9/11 had not happened, the world would be an entirely different place. 9/11 gave the present US administration the opportunity to invade Afghanistan. The Taliban are a very rigid, severe, fundamentalist Islamic regime, very hard to live with, but they were not, on the whole, terrorists. Now, having been defeated in the fighting in Afghanistan, they have regrouped and have come back, learning all the ways of terrorism. They are now terrorists, and they go into Iraq, which is wide open for anyone who wants to create mayhem.

An entire nation of terrorists has been created in Afghanistan quite unnecessarily. The attack on Iraq is a terrible tragedy for the world. They are now on the very brink of civil war. In fact, there is a small-scale civil war going on at this time. It is not all over the country, thankfully, at the moment, but it is civil war nevertheless. I think there is no kind of war more terrible than civil war.

During the Spanish civil war, one side of a street would support Franco and the other side of the street would be for the Republican government. They would fight and kill each other, just as was done more recently in Kosovo and Bosnia in the Balkans under the auspices of Slobodan Milosevic, then President of Serbia.

The world has come to a point not only of no return but of total crisis, total confrontation between good and ill, between that which produces harmony and that which produces the opposite. This is the result of the energy of the Sword of Cleavage. In the Christian Bible we read that Jesus said, "The father shall be divided against the son, and the son against his father", and so on, all very destructive. The Sword of Cleavage is, ironically it may seem, the energy of Love. That is what has been happening and is happening today, and will be focused to a fine point by Maitreya.

It is the energy of Love pouring out now through all the planes. It saturates the world, and its effect on humanity is to make you more of what you are. If you are a person of goodwill, that will be stimulated and potentised. If you are destructive, of bad will, you become more so. All, good and bad alike, are stimulated.

In this way humanity will see very clearly what it has to do. If this did not happen, we might feel that we could soldier on as we are. It would be difficult, but we might think that eventually, perhaps, things would subside and be all right again – as it never was in the past. The Sword of Cleavage sharpens the differences and makes clear the options before humanity. More and more people, with the sharpened vision that the Sword gives us, see that there is no alternative any more to peace. If we do not have peace, we will have complete destruction of all life on the planet.

Peace, then, is no longer an option for humanity: it is essential. This understanding is the result of the action of Maitreya's energy of Love. It is the Sword of Cleavage, outlining clearly the way forward for humanity: through brotherhood, justice, sharing and peace; through freedom, right relationship and all that flows from these. It is either that, or continuing on the way of the present and destroying all life.

Maitreya's Sword of Cleavage brings this black and white confrontation before humanity so that we see it clearly, sharply, with no woolly edges. We take one side or the other. We take the way of right human relationship, of construction and harmony, on the one hand, or the way of wrong human relations and eventually total destruction for everyone, on the other.

It is so important that before another election everybody in this country [USA] must insist on a completely different voting system. You should not accept the voting system of the last two elections. These I know with certainty were more fraudulent than those of any 'banana republic'. They were outrageous, for you and the world, and something that you should never allow your government to do again.

There has to be a voting system with proof of your signature. That must be for every single vote. No machinery should be allowed to usurp the handwritten vote; none of the dodges that were used massively in the last election. Everybody knew that the vast majority of young people wanted change and would vote for Kerry. So in many places, they were grouped together in special rooms and not allowed to join the queues that were waiting to cast their votes. They were kept there for hours. If you keep youngsters of 18, 19 or 20 years of age for hours, waiting to vote, they do not stay. They drifted away in droves.

Such practices were widespread. It is so simple: you just keep the young away. Someone is denied those votes, perhaps thousands of votes, that could be crucial if the vote is close. It is a very simple, very effective ruse.

"Unfortunately, as recent history shows, this is not the case, even in those countries which lay great stress on the probity of their election process."

No country is more on the *qui vive* about the probity of other countries' elections than the United States. The election has to be not only fair but 'democratic'. It must be 'democratic', otherwise it is deemed unfair, automatically illegal.

Hamas was elected by a perfectly fair legal system of representational votes and became the freely elected government of the Palestinians. The United States administration refused to recognise or deal with Hamas. Israel (a lackey of the US) refuses to deal with the representatives of Hamas because they say it is not democratic. How much more democratic could it be than when the vast majority of people of the country voted for them? It was a landslide, almost 90 per cent. What can you do against such duplicity and double standards in the affairs of state?

Diversity of democratic forms

There are many forms, many types of democracy. The US administration thinks that the only legal election is one between two political parties. That is the case in Europe, Japan and elsewhere, but there are many different ideas of democracy, degrees and types of democracy.

China would claim to be a democratic country, very different from the democracy of Britain, America, France,

Germany and Scandinavia. If you were to ask the average, educated Chinese person, especially on the eastern seaboard, if their government is democratic, they would probably say: "Yes it is. It is a form of democracy. I am free to do what I want. I can do this job or that job. There is no compulsion to do certain work. I can do whatever job I am good at and trained for, without restriction. We have democracy."

It is not what we would call democracy, but it is a form of democracy, a mixed democracy. The Chinese are presenting to the world a very interesting form of government, which is an experiment and may not end up in the way it seems to be going. That is the nature of experiment. These experiments on the scale of a country like China take time to unfold. In China you have a group of strong men with the army and police behind them, so they can enforce what would be the rule of law as they see the law, and they do enforce it. It is a 1st-ray country. The soul of the country is 1st-ray; the personality is 3rd-ray.** They are not very sentimental. That is not one of their faults.

This country [USA], as devious and autocratic as your present government is, has a 2nd-ray soul and a 6th-ray personality, and is sentimental to a degree. However, I would rather have that than the more robust, to put it mildly, form of the Chinese democracy, because I think the 2nd-ray soul of America will eventually manifest itself, and the sooner the better for the world.

The world is really waiting for the soul of America to manifest. When it does, it will take to heart the needs of the world as a whole. For the first time it will broaden its viewpoint under the influence of the teaching of Maitreya, Who will invoke the soul aspect of America, and inspire America to share the resources that it has in such abundance. A new Marshall Plan on a world scale will be the result. That is one of the most hopeful things to hold before you as members of this nation. The American nation is a great nation. It has done some terrible things, but so have all the nations. It is a young nation, so in a sense it is to be expected

24

that it gets out of hand at times; but it is so powerful, so big, so rich, that it has an enormous influence in the world.

That influence is the natural outflow of the intelligence and inventiveness of its people. It is also a planned influence, planned from Washington, from the White House and the Pentagon – which is the real seat of power in America. The Pentagon and the White House control the destinies of America and to some extent the destinies of the world. This should not be.

The American Empire

It is the task of Maitreya to control the will to power of the present administration and the urge to develop a worldwide 'democratic' system, which will be to all intents and purposes an American Empire. There are many Americans who are quite consciously thinking of and working towards the establishment of the American Empire. They call this century the 'American Century' in which this empire will come to be. That is their will and plan, but it will not be. It is not the plan of the Logos of our planet that any one nation or one form of government dominates throughout the world.

Between the 17th and 20th centuries, Britain established a power worldwide and formed what is no longer an empire. It did form an empire, which it then gave up last century, but it formed something much more lasting and meaningful, the Commonwealth of Nations.

The Commonwealth of Nations is one of the real acts of coming together of peoples for the long-term Plan of our Planetary Logos, and therefore of the Spiritual Hierarchy, Who carry out the Plan.

The Commonwealth of Nations is not really a common wealth at all, but it instituted a freedom of trading that had not been seen before. It is not the same among other nations but does pertain around the Commonwealth. Nowadays many Australians find it difficult to salute the Queen, salute the flag, as many see themselves as totally distinct and separate. Nevertheless, there are millions of Australians who have a blood tie to the home country of Britain. That is true of every Commonwealth country: New Zealand, Canada, the West Indies, parts of Africa, India, Pakistan, and so on.

If you looked at a map before the last war, most of it was pink. That meant it was part of the Commonwealth of Nations, the former British Empire. The empire is no more and parts of it, mainly in Africa, are struggling to find their feet as individual nations.

The Commonwealth of Nations, who have kept these invisible ties to the home country of Great Britain, are really presenting a view of gatherings of people, of different colours, different traditions, different religions, different ways of thinking and feeling and relating, living together in peace. In Britain today all these are coming together, often in large groups.

You can go to Manchester or some other city and large groups have Pakistani or West Indian names, traditions, foods, religion, but they have English accents and see themselves as British. They look different but they sound the same, and they are all British.

They live together in relative peace in a way which is quite unique in the world. There are 'flare-ups' when the British National Party [extreme right-wing party] gets nasty and sets itself against the Pakistanis, for example, and the Pakistanis fight back, but it is rare and happens only every few years. Broadly speaking, there is an amazing goodwill and cementing of good relationships among these quite separate communities. They do not mix, on the whole. Some do, of course, but on the whole each nationality from whatever part of the Commonwealth keeps its own identity, has its own language, its own food, its own schools, its own churches or temples. They are distinct, they are friendly with one another, and there is the minimum of friction.

Three experiments

The British Commonwealth of Nations is in miniature (although we are talking about millions of people) an experiment. There are three major experiments that are being carried out in the world. That one is Britain.

Here, in America, it is the bringing of Europe to America, taking a part of Europe and putting it overseas. That is largely how 'America' came to be: a sample of most of the people of Europe – not many French because of their ray difference, English, Irish, Scots, Dutch, Germans, Spanish, Scandinavians, especially the Swedes, Italians, Greeks and a few more from elsewhere. You just picked them up and put them down in America, and told them: "Now get on, colonise this country, get over the Rockies, find El Dorado, California."

'Democracy' and slavery

Then a great mistake was made. People talk about democracy as a wonderful thing, and of how it goes back to the Greeks.

The Greeks were the first democrats, it is true. From the 5th century BC it did have democracy of a kind, a democratic council, a meeting of like-minded men at the same social level, all senators, landholders, all rich, powerful men in Athens. But Athens, like other Greek cities, and like Roman cities, was run totally on the backs of slaves. Slavery existed long before Athens, but Athens rose to power on the backs of slaves. So, too, did the Greek civilisation, from which so much has come, so many intelligent discoveries, especially in science, geometry, architecture, and so on. We have learned so much from these extraordinarily wise and gifted men, but they did all of that on the backs of slaves.

Athens and the other major cities of Greece were run by slaves. You went out, fought battles, conquered, and took prisoners. The prisoners were brought home as slaves. When this country, America, waxed in power and riches, the same thing happened. You got your slaves this time from Africa. The Arabs had been slave traders for generations before that. They ran their economies on slave labour, some of them still do, and some of the potential slaves themselves sold others to the slave traders. They took part in this awful trade in human beings. They got richer so they could get out of the lowest caste. It was always the poorest and lowest in the social system who became slaves. The southern part of this country, as you know, was built on slavery, and a large part of the wealth of this country came from slavery.

A large part of the wealth still enjoyed by the aristocracy and sub-aristocracy of Britain was gained from selling slaves. They owned the ships that went down to the African coast, the Gold Coast, the Ivory Coast, and other areas. There they bought and traded slaves to ship across the sea. It was a terrible trade, and has continued until today: slaves are still bought and sold in parts of Africa, India, China, and other countries.

There are many different types of democracy or democratic countries. A democracy based on slavery is a contradiction in terms, unless you can divide humanity into two different kinds of people. Those who have power can make the semblance of democratic law at their level, but at the same time it can be built on a deeply entrenched slave economy. It is tragic. This is the way humanity has behaved for countless millennia.

The Security Council

Despite the strength of the American voice calling for democracy everywhere (and I am personally very much in favour of democracy), there is no country more vociferous in demanding democracy outside the US than the United States itself. Furthermore, as my Master has pointed out, this country is curiously blind to the lack of democracy that exists in the United Nations.

The action of the Security Council is the exact opposite of democracy. The Security Council was brought into being by the five nations who had the atomic bomb – Britain, America, France, China and Russia. Because they had the atomic bomb, these five dominated the actions of the United

Nations and formed the Security Council, which gave them the right of veto.

Nothing is so against democracy as having within it a veto. Any country that has the veto can use it to prevent the implementation of any resolution made by the United Nations General Assembly as a whole. The USA uses the veto more than any other nation and has used it 63 times in the case of resolutions against Israel. Israel just 'cocks a snook' at the United Nations because it knows the American veto keeps it immune to criticism.

One of the excuses for attacking Iraq used by America and Britain was that Saddam Hussein was negligent in implementing 19 (some say 17) resolutions of the United Nations. The resolutions were about weapons of mass destruction. The US and UK claimed that Iraq had not destroyed its weapons, which in fact it had done, as we now know, as *Share International* magazine knew and published before the war started. Israel, however, goes scot-free. It need not try to implement any of the 63 resolutions still standing against it, because of the veto system and US protection.

The veto and the Security Council have outlasted their usefulness, their reason for being, and must go. The United Nations must be purified of the veto and become a truly democratic assembly. It cannot be a democratic assembly until the Security Council is dissolved and the power of the veto withdrawn. Then the voice, which my Master calls "the voice of the hope of the world", the United Nations General Assembly itself, can be heard purely and simply, and be used to set to rights the world as quickly as possible. That is a very urgent matter indeed.

Despite the present Western focus on democracy everywhere and at all cost, whether people want it or not, if it does not follow the type of democracy that pertains in the USA it is not considered to be democracy, and therefore is seen as some form of authoritarian government.

Democrats tend to resent any kind of diminution of their democracy, but despite the present focus, the day is coming when democrats everywhere will not resent a degree of Hierarchical oversight and decision making. Once people have come to trust the wisdom and higher knowledge of the Masters, Their oversight will be welcomed as a learning process. A new and rare state of humility will bring this about.

When we see the Masters and realise how tolerant They are, we will begin to see that we are not at all tolerant. We will see that the Masters never impose Their will on humanity. When we see how patient They are, and how closely They work within the Law in everything They do, we will see that the higher knowledge, the wisdom of the Masters, is something we would love to have.

Global warming

There are people today who are so sensitive to their little power and knowledge, they think they could run a world. There are some who think that they know everything – scientists, for example.

There are scientists who say that this planet is heating up, that global warming is a reality and we have to do something about it. We are pouring all this rubbish into the atmosphere, and it is heating up the planet. At the same time there are other scientists saying the very opposite; they tend to be in the USA.

There are scientists here who have been suborned, or who genuinely think that this claim of the planet heating up is not really true. They believe it is not going to be solved simply by making manufacturers curb their excess gas emissions. That will not do it, and it is not even necessary to do it, they say. There are other solutions. In time, they say, we will have all the oil we want when we get our hands on the Iraqi oil, the Venezuelan oil, and any oil that is around not actually being used. We will stock it up. We have mountains that are carved out, hollow inside. We will put all the oil inside in barrels. It will do until Kingdom Come, they believe, and, being mainly fundamentalists, they know that Kingdom Come is nearer than most people think.

The time is coming when people will be glad if a Master says: "Well, if I were you, I would do it this way." They will love it. They will become like little boys at school. The Masters know so much. They have access to any information They need. They just set the Devas on it.

People will be very glad to receive the guidance and a degree of control from the point of view of advice – what policy to take, how to go along the lines of the Plan. We do not know the Plan. We did not know until we saw the Masters that there was a Plan; but there is a Plan, and the Masters carry out the Plan. Since we do not know that there is a Plan we do anything except the right thing. We do the right thing by accident and everything else by choice.

There will be a degree of oversight that will be perfectly acceptable even by people who are very rigid. One of the things people say about 'this story' is: "I do not like the word 'Masters'." I say: "Well, They are Masters over Themselves. They are Masters in the sense that They have complete awareness and complete control on every plane of our planet. That is what makes a Master." And they say: "I still do not like it. I do not like Them being ..." What they really mean is being 'above' us. They think that Masters, being Who They are, inevitably will tell us what to do. They do not know that Masters will only tell people what they can do when They are asked. Ask a Master what would be the right thing to do and He may say: "Well, the wise thing to do would be such and such." If you are wise, you will do that because it will be right. But otherwise They will not say. They are in a purely advisory relationship with us.

Spiritual groups

There are many spiritual groups in this country and elsewhere, many thousands of them. However glamoured they might be, inactive, inward looking, however little they take note of the world as a whole, they do exist. They are at the moment almost completely separated, fragmented. Few of them have any relationship with any others.

When I came to this country for the first time, in January 1980, for the Unity in Diversity Council Conference, I thought: "Hallelujah, this is a wonderful group. It brings together groups of all kinds. They are working together under one umbrella called the Unity in Diversity Council, the greatest diversity and the utmost unity, a marvellous concept, to me the concept of true living on planet Earth." That is what we need – the greatest variety and diversity, all the different countries giving their qualities to the whole because of their different ray structures. The rays give the qualities, and the countries can, therefore, pour into the common pool all that they distinctly and uniquely have because of their soul and personality ray combination.

All are needed, all have a destined part to play in the world. More and more, as the age of Aquarius progresses and the Masters have been in the world a long time, nations will be demonstrating the qualities of their rays, their individual gifts, and giving that for the benefit of the whole. That is as it should be. Today it is not so, but that is as it will be.

Groups like this need to work together with other groups, to support all such groups in building world public opinion. It is world public opinion, as it expresses itself through the peoples of the world, which will change the world.

Maitreya's task is to galvanise world public opinion and focus it through a few simple ideas, so that people everywhere are calling for justice, for freedom; for sharing as the only way to achieve justice and the end of war, the creation of peace. Peace and the end of terrorism are dependent on the creation of justice, and only one thing will accomplish that: sharing the resources of the world.

These are the simple things that humanity has to grasp. There are millions of groups. Some are calling for more justice for the animals, the end of abattoirs, "vegetarianism for all", and so on. "End the killing of the animal kingdom."

"Save the whales." "Save the seals." These are great ideals. I am all for them, but you cannot have humanity in their millions promoting all these different ideas at the same time. It simply weakens their impact.

It needs to be simple: the transformation of humanity through sharing the resources, so creating justice, and so creating peace. That is the idea for all the groups throughout the world to focus on. Peace is no longer an option: we have no alternative. That has to be understood, because if there is no peace then eventually we will destroy ourselves. A small war would become a big war. It would become a nuclear war and all the nations would disappear.

I am not writing your banner headlines at the moment. I am trying to focus your minds on the essentials: sharing, leading to justice, leading inevitably to the end of terrorism, and to world peace. Only that will do it. As Maitreya says: "There is no other course." If we do not share, then we die, sooner or later. It is as simple as that.

It is a question of sharing and transformation of the world. That creates the trust upon which all future agreements are based. You can solve anything if there is trust. You have to create the trust, and only sharing the resources of the world will do that. Then all the other problems – the Middle East, the problems of saving the planet itself, and so on – all of that can be dealt with when there is trust. Most of the disagreements will just disappear, dissipated in the goodwill that will flow out in tremendous potency when sharing of the resources takes place.

An important and useful task for this group and all groups of this kind is to act consciously at creating synthesis, at developing unity in diversity with other groups. Look on the internet. Find out by reading the websites of all the groups. I should think there is not a reasonably-sized group today that does not have a website. There you can read about various groups, and if they share our concerns and values, if they work for the good of the world, then it is worthwhile contacting them and making some kind of demonstration at fairs and festivals, or exchanging speakers. Working with other groups is possible. It is difficult, but it is possible. We have had very little success in Britain, but perhaps we have not tried very hard.

All people are seeking Unity. That is why they join or form themselves into groups. At the same time, everyone wants to express his or her individuality, that unique quality of every incarnated soul. Only the kind of Unity that is natural and organic, without prejudice and rigidity, can form a proper framework for that rich diversity which makes planet Earth so interesting a home for its people.***

[*For more detailed discussions on Maitreya's Priorities, see *Maitreya's Mission, Volume Three,* Chapter 1.]

[**For the discussion on the Seven Rays and Rays of Nations, see *Maitreya's Mission, Volume One*, Chapter 6 and *Volume Two*, Chapter 13.]

[***Readers are encouraged to read the articles and questions and answers on Unity published in *The Art of Co-operation,* Part Three, 'Unity'. They focus on the need for unity as the aim of life and the achievement of unity in group work.]

DIVERSITY AND INDIVIDUALITY

Q. What is the relationship between diversity and individuality? Can the one exist without the other? (March 2007)

A. If there were no individuality, you would not be talking about any relationship or diversity – no individuality, no nothing. We are individuals. That is our God-given being. The thing is to get that individuality under control. Do not impose it on groups. Do not impose it on other people. You must never give up your individuality, but you put it at the service of the group. You have something to give that nobody else can give, and they have something to give that nobody else has to give. Everybody, from their very individuality, has something that no one else can give. That is the diversity of the group.

Every person is unique. That is your individuality; it comes from your soul. You are individualised human souls and each soul is unique. In the whole manifested universe there is not another soul like your soul. It has its unique vibration that a Master can recognise instantly. This is something which nobody can take away from you, and you should not allow anyone to take away from you. That individuality should be accepted as part of the diversity of a group.

Everyone has a right to say what they think and others have a right to disagree. In the end the group as a whole has to come to a unity, which in practical terms is a consensus. The group consensus comes not by taking votes – who votes for this or that – but by a consensus of thought that inculcates group thinking. This is what we are trying to do because only in that way can we correctly work with the energy of Aquarius. It has no individual application. It works only through groups, and that is the whole point in forming groups.

Groups are forming now in every department of life because people sense that we are entering a time in which the groups count. Until the present, a group of individual people – but not a group – followed a person who was the leader. Today it is different and tomorrow it will be even more different. The position of the leader will gradually disappear and the group as a whole will foster maximum diversity with unity, and come to its decisions by consensus.

There are people who do not believe in consensus. They say there is no such thing: "You win some and you lose some." That is the voice of the modern businessman. It is a game of competition. You judge yourself by how many you win and how many you failed to win. Group work has nothing at all to do with winning or losing, nothing to do with competition. It is consensus of thought in a group. It is not overcoming the minds of others and shouting the loudest.

Q. In the process of group decision-making there is often a diversity of opinion but no unity. In this case would you please comment on how to come to a decision? (March 2007)

A. If there is a diversity of opinion in group decision-making, that is only to be expected. If you have a diverse group, you have diverse opinions – not perhaps as totally diverse as in another group – but you must accept that there will be different opinions.

The beauty of group work is in coming to a consensus. Accept that there will be differences, look forward to it. It is part of life. Enjoy it. You want diverse viewpoints. You also want unifying ways of addressing them. Use both methods. You get people to say their piece and hear them all. Some will stand out as being more meaningful, more practical, more readily able to be implemented. Do that and let the fanciful ones drop to the bottom. It is all trial and error. I do not know ways to do things that you do not know. You know just as well as I do.

Q. Unity through diversity is our chance to allow the energy of synthesis to work outwardly with other groups. We also realised that unity through diversity has to be implemented inwardly in our own groups. Unity through diversity is to be implemented everywhere. (January/February 2002)

A. I quite agree. The aim of our life, whether we have realised it or not, is the establishment of unity, representing the unity that already exists. Every atom in the manifested universe is interrelated with every other atom.

Unity is not simply an idea that we can hold or not hold. It is driving us on our evolutionary process. This evolution, expansion of consciousness, must be a process of ever-widening awareness of unity and a synthesis of all the possible aspects of unity that exist until you have the 'Mind of God', seeing the unity that underlies the whole of existence.

My own idea of unity is of the utmost possible diversity. As you know, there are seven rays of energy, and these in their various relationships produce all the phenomena that we see and experience. Because of the interaction of the rays, there is infinite diversity. All the nations are governed on the soul and personality levels by one of the seven rays. In this way nations are quite varied in their qualities.

My understanding of the Master's article on 'Unity' [page 149] is that it is not only to do with group work. Although He does relate the article to the workings of groups, He also relates it to the world scene. He is really talking about international relationships and the need for unity in that area; that is the urgency. Your own group relationships need the understanding and growth of unity, but they do not have the same effect on the world as, for example, Mr George W. Bush's lack of a sense of the unity necessary to produce co-operation and so solve the problems of the world. Only through a sense of unity can one work co-operatively.

We know that the most efficient exponents of competition, the opposite of co-operation, have been

America, the various countries of Europe, Japan, Australia and Canada. A very limited number of countries are, in fact, 'running the show'. The world is complex. Therefore, the problems involved in its development, even maintaining its physical existence, demand co-operation and peace, the ability to work together to solve problems that are threatening the very existence of the world. These are the real problems that the Master is talking about in this article on unity.

The Master relates the article to the groups because He has various groups under His charge. He is developing the ideas in relation to both the groups and the international scene because the groups relate to the world. The effects on the groups are relatively unimportant compared with the effects that unity or competition have on the world, on our international relations. If, for example, America had signed the Kyoto Protocol for the stabilisation of greenhouse gas emissions, it would have been a good idea not only because 180 nations saw it as a good idea – and, I have no doubt, many Americans did too – but because Mr Bush stands for that approach. But he stands for a Republican approach to that problem. Historically this has been whatever is seen as being in the best interest of the country they represent, the United States. The representatives of every country at any given time are no doubt looking after the most crucial interests of their nation as they see it. Some nations are a little more advanced, have a little more soul involvement in their consciousness, and so look on a broader scale. They are able to see not only their own personal interests but can take a wider view from time to time, and that is good and useful. So it depends on the point of evolution reached, and on the importance of the idea or problem.

Diversity is the fundamental nature of the life of humanity. The individuality of every human being is not only a fact; it is one of the great facts of human evolution. Individuality shows the uniqueness of every person. As an extension of the individual, every nation is a soul with a personality. Either the personality ray or the soul ray is uppermost, more influential.

Unfortunately, at the present time, the soul ray is hidden for the most part by the activity of the lesser ray, the personality ray, and most nations just look after their own personal interests so far as they can. If they are big, powerful nations like the United States or the Europeans, they look after their own interests more effectively than small nations who do not have the clout, internationally, to make their voices heard or have any effect on the whole.

The greatest diversity within the greatest unity, or put the other way, the greatest unity with the greatest diversity, is the ideal that humanity is seeking, and is in alignment with the Plan of our Logos for the development of this world. Maitreya in one of His early messages [Message No. 3] said, "Allow Me to show you the way forward, into a simpler life where no man lacks; where no two days are alike; where the joy of Brotherhood manifests through all men."

"Where no two days are alike" is, to me, an extraordinary statement. The only people for whom no two days are alike are young children and the rare person who has enough money and leisure to do what he wants to do, in which he can fill his life creatively, moment to moment, so that there is no drudgery. Boredom and drudgery come out of sameness. In unity there is no sameness. It is not about the repetition of like ideas time and again until it gets boring. It is creatively seeing life and, therefore, every aspect, every movement, of that life creatively, newly, moment to moment. When you are in the state of unity that the Master is talking about, that is the state of timeless, creative existence which exists for us all.

Q. Are awareness of others and co-ordination with others prerequisites for achieving unity in diversity? What other qualities and steps would you recommend to effect unity among diverse people and groups? (March 2007)

A. You have to find a way. It is not my way you want. I do not have ready-made ways that you can take. It is not like that. You want the way that works for you with your group. Your group has to experiment. Use different ways. Use your own gifts.

Q. What is the difference between diversity and fragmentation? (March 2007)

A. Fragmentation is formless. Diversity within a unity is not formless. The form is the outcome of the unity. Fragmentation by itself has no outer form or unity.

With unity in diversity, the diverse groups and points of view are not fragments of the whole; they are part of the whole. The whole is the outcome of their coming together and that gives form. The unity comes out of the diversity, not the other way around. You do not have the unity and then the diversity. You have diversity and then a growing unity by being able to overcome differences, to aim at a unified approach, a unified thought pattern. You attain a degree of group consciousness. That creates a form, which we call unity.

Everyone is longing for unity. Everyone is driving themselves towards unity. That is why people join groups, why they join political parties. They are looking for like-minded people with whom they can become unified. The aim of all life is to become unified. In the Age of Aquarius, this coming Age, you will see this manifested through the energy of Synthesis. It will blend humanity together into a veritable synthesis, a real unity.

Every nation, every people within the nation, with their diverse and different points of view, their different sense of the meaning and purpose of life, will give individual expression to that purpose. In this way, a huge tapestry is formed of all the ideas and creativity of all the different nations under the different rays. They have different rays to bring this huge panoply of qualities into one great unity. This unity is in the mind of the Logos and we are carrying out His Plan, whether consciously or not. It happens because it is planned. It is the nature of the Plan of the Logos to have the greatest definition of the individuality of the different nations, each one expressing its own unique quality that is instantly recognisable and different from all others. But eventually all will become part of a fused and blended whole. It is a fusion and blending of difference, not a fusion of the same. A fusion of the same is what America would have by everybody adopting their version of democracy, as if they had the final answer to the development of political systems in democracy. But the Plan is that each nation will carry out its own destiny, and a unity will evolve out of all that diversity.

If you have a garden and every flower is white, it is a nice garden but rather boring. A garden that has only one colour of flower would not be a true garden. But a garden where you feel that all the colours are presenting themselves, and is so arranged that it beautifully leads from one part to another, is a real garden, uplifting and refreshing.

Some painters paint in one colour or maybe different tones of one colour. You have unity but it is a kind of spurious unity. You can do that occasionally. But if all your pictures were one colour, and all the same, you would have unity but no diversity. In the same way it is the diversity of human beings that is interesting.

Q. Among Maitreya's priorities is "the removal of guilt and fear". You have talked about fear.* Would you please talk about the removal and overcoming of guilt? (March 2007)

A. Guilt and fear are very much related. Guilt is the result of fear. The fundamental situation that creates fear also creates guilt. The fear is that you have sinned. It is the result of wrong teaching by the Christian groups for 2,000 years, which has instilled fear and guilt into 1,000 million Christian people. In every incarnation they meet the same thing – fear instilling guilt and guilt instilling fear, and the terrible effect on the sense of self-esteem that such teaching has. That, together with countless and age-old superstitions that fill the minds of people of other religious traditions, makes fear and guilt a powerful blockage on the way to awakening consciousness.

A large part of Maitreya's time will be taken up in removing fear and guilt from humanity. He will not simply manipulate it and get rid of it but His teaching is fashioned to remove fear and guilt. He has given you the way; you know it already. The way to remove fear and guilt is to practise the three techniques that Maitreya suggests. Instil, acquire, build into yourself honesty of mind, sincerity of spirit, and detachment. If done assiduously, correctly, these inevitably build the detachment in which fear and guilt disappear.

If you are detached, you are free of guilt and fear. It could not be otherwise. Guilt and fear exist out of attachment. If you are attached to your beliefs – Christian, Muslim or Buddhist – and you do things that are against your beliefs, you live in guilt and fear. For example, Roman Catholics are told that they should not have sex outside marriage, and that even within marriage they should not use contraception. Yet millions of Catholics do that, and they live in the guilt instilled by their action.

For Roman Catholics, this is a tremendous inner struggle. Should they obey the stipulations of the Church underwritten by the Pope that you should not have sex outside marriage, that you cannot be married twice in a church, that contraception is a sin? If Roman Catholics believe what the Pope says, they are in trouble because their common sense tells them this is not wrong or sinful. It is natural and normal. They have the guilt and fear of retribution instilled in them.

Maitreya will remove this guilt and fear from humanity by talking common sense. You can remove it from yourself by practising detachment. It is all to do with detachment. If you are attached to your retribution because of your fear of retribution, you feel guilty. If you are not attached, there is no fear, there is no guilt.

Some actions are wrong, but they can be righted. The Law of Karma rights all actions. It is a great beneficent Law. When you do a wrong that is destructive, it is changed by the effect that you have brought on yourself through the Law of Karma. It is an effect, not retribution.

The Law of Karma does not make you guilty. It just gives you a simple Law: "As you sow, so shall you reap." You have thoughts, you have actions. The effects stemming from these causes that you have set in motion make a life for good or ill. Some of it will be good, some of it will be painful. But we have done it ourselves. There is no such thing as retribution. There is karma, which is the Law balancing itself: "As you sow, so shall you reap." By making it possible for people to truly understand the Law of Karma, Maitreya will make it real for them. They will see that the best action is harmless action because in that way you reap harmless results, creative results, good results. You have good karma.

[*See *Maitreya's Mission, Volume Two,* Chapter 10, 'The Overcoming of Fear'.]

Q. You have said that there is no sin, but what about greed, selfishness, jealousy, racism etc, all crimes of separativeness? Aren't they all a sign of a lack of evolution? (October 2010)

A. Yes, indeed, but when I talk about sin I mean it in the non-Christian sense. Christians talk about sins and the devil tempting us. But it is nothing to do with that. From the Masters' point of view, the only 'sin' is that of separation or separativeness. That is the sin from which all others emerge.

Q. (1) Is it possible to develop one's heart? (2) How can I become more responsive to others, to the world, from my heart? (January/February 2006)

A. (1) Yes. (2) Meditate more. Serve more. Learn to recognise the difference between an emotional (solar plexus) response and a spiritual heart centre response. Cultivate sensitivity to the latter. Cultivate inclusiveness. Try not to shy away from unpleasant or painful facts. Try not to be complacent. Try not to be afraid or ashamed to express love if experienced.

Q. How can one open the mind more – become less rigid or set in one's beliefs? (November 2008)

A. Become more tolerant of difference. Meet more people of opposing views and try to understand their point of view.

Q. Maitreya has said, "Without self-esteem you can do nothing." So, what are tiny ways in which a person can increase his or her self-esteem if it is low? (June 2009)

A. Achievement, of any kind, in any direction, increases self-esteem. Therefore all effort should be addressed to the achieving of some goal, large or small, and then steadily 'upping' the goal until the confidence that comes with achievement becomes steady and reliable.

Aspiration is the key. If we can inspire the latent aspiration in ourselves and others, self-worth and self-esteem automatically follow.

THREE HIERARCHICAL EXPERIMENTS:
USA, UK AND RUSSIA

Q. In your talk you discussed the British Commonwealth and a form of unity in diversity with a role to play in the Plan of the Logos. You also mentioned the USA in this respect. In **The Externalisation of the Hierarchy** *the Master Djwhal Khul states that the USSR as a great Federation of Republics is the future synthesis. Could you please elaborate on the*

British Commonwealth, the USA and the former USSR, and the Plan of the Logos? (March 2007)

A. There are three aspects of the Plan: one in Britain, one in America, and one in Russia. In the talk I went into the role of Britain. I did not get round to talking about Russia, so this question is very relevant. A similar kind of experiment is being carried out in Russia.

In America it is very simple. All the European nations were just lifted up and deposited in America. It became a mixture of all these different groups and out of that something entirely different eventually will come. You can tell an American a mile away. Why? There is something about an American face that is not in Europe. It is the amalgam of all these different groups: Teutonic and Latin, African, Native American, South American, and so on all coming together in America. All these different racial types and groups mixed together, and out of that has come something that you have never seen before.

Today it is not just a physical mix. For the Masters that would not be all that important. The Masters look on the physical as the lowest aspect. What They are interested in is the psychic aspect, the evolution of consciousness, and of different types and aspects of consciousness in different peoples.

Humanity is evolving all the time according to the Plan of evolution in the mind of the Logos. Hierarchy, through its higher members such as the Christ and the Buddha, have an entry into the mind of the Logos, and know the Plan. Their work is to make the Plan work out through humanity and the lower kingdoms.

The experiment is threefold, which makes it very potent. It is potentised by being a triangle. There is one point of the triangle in Britain, one in America, and the third in Russia.

In Britain, it is the Commonwealth of Nations, the grouping of many nations of the world into one little country. All the members of the Commonwealth are brought together, keeping their own existence and identity. The different groups stay together and do not on the whole mix, but relatively peacefully, they co-exist.

In this experiment taking place, Russia is the third aspect. What was the Soviet Union brought together about 280 million people on a sixth of the world's surface stretching from St Petersburg in the west to Vladivostok in the east. It was a colossal country made up of many different peoples: European nations of western Russia, the people around the Black Sea area, through Kazakhstan and Uzbekistan, through the Islamic peoples of eastern Russia right to Vladivostok. It is an extraordinary mixture.

The former Soviet Union is now broken up (as predicted by Maitreya, published in *Share International* and sent as press releases to the world's media in January 1990), and it has come about almost by stealth. Now there is a federation of autonomous and semi-autonomous states. Some of them are still struggling to be autonomous. They made up what was the homogenised Soviet Union under a group of dictators, strong men in Moscow, and the Communist party, which was only about 10 million. Ten million people roughly were allowed to join the Communist Party. That little group imposed their will on the 270 million people in the Soviet Union, aiming at equality but forgetting freedom. The government in Moscow would still like to have more control over events in other parts of what was the Soviet Union, no doubt. But they are national, independent states.

America, too, is really a federation of states with a fair degree of autonomy. There is federal law and state law, and these are not always the same. The states guard their individual identity very jealously and by no means are subject solely to federal law. They have a large say in the running of the country.

In what was the former Soviet Union, the independent members of the federation have, theoretically, a complete say on how their state is run, although Western Russia and Moscow still have a measure of control over some of the less developed states. And there is also a great deal of infighting at the local political level to maintain or overthrow that old

Communist regime. Some people are still Communist at heart. It is a process that will take a long time to resolve.

If you look at the constitution of Russia and that of America, they are so similar it is extraordinary. They believe in all the same things. They are both 6th-ray countries. They each think they have freedom. They each think they have justice because their theoretical aim is freedom and justice. In America there is a degree of freedom but little social justice. In Russia under the Soviets there was a degree of social justice but no freedom. They set about it in different ways because of their different traditions. They will slowly come to understand that without freedom you cannot have justice; without justice you cannot have freedom. They are one and the same.

These are the three groupings along the evolutionary plan for the development of humanity, so that there will be the greatest integration with the greatest diversity. All these three great experiments – America, Britain and the federated states of Russia – are aiming at unity in diversity in their own different way. That is how the Plan works out.

Of course, there is a great interchange between these nations. As a triangle the forces, the energies of Hierarchy, flow through all three of them. They are the three most important groupings in the world for the next approximately 2,500 years and they will bring about a complete transformation of humanity. The rays or the energies of these countries will bring about change: in Britain the energy of the 2nd Ray of Love/Wisdom of its soul and the 1st Ray of Power or Government on the personality level; in America the 2nd Ray of Love/Wisdom from the soul level, the 6th Ray of Idealism or Devotion on the personality level; and in Russia the 7th Ray of Organisation or Ritual from the soul level and the 6th Ray of Idealism or Devotion on the personality level.* These rays will play through these three groups. From time to time people of other nations will incarnate into the British, the American, the Russian groups, and, in due course, this will bring about a unification of the world, with the maximum of diversity and freedom for all the peoples.

[*For discussion on the seven rays and the rays of nations, see *Maitreya's Mission, Volume One*, Chapter 6, and *Maitreya's Mission, Volume Two*, Chapter 13.]

Q. What is the purpose of these different developments? (March 2007)

A. Every race has seven sub-races, and all nations today are part of the fifth root race. Europe and America represent the fifth sub-race of the fifth root race. From among these people, especially in America, is slowly being drawn the nucleus of the sixth sub-race of the fifth root race. The fifth sub-race expresses the 5th-ray quality of lower concrete mind. This has produced the advancement of our technological science. The sixth sub-race will give expression eventually to that higher aspect of mind we call intuition.

That which we generally know as science is, from the Masters' point of view, the activity of the lower mind, but by lower They do not mean less. It is simply the lower aspect of the mind using the brain and creating the science of today, concrete science.

There are three types of science. There is concrete science or technology. There is the science of the higher mind – philosophical, theoretical and abstract – the science of Einstein, for example. There is also the science of the psyche or white magic, which the Masters use. It is the same science as the others but is intangible, although you can see its results.

A Master comes into a room. How did He come through the wall? He suddenly appears. He does it by white magic, and He suddenly disappears by the same science. He creates something in His hand – or Sai Baba creates vibhuti when you hold out your hand. It is the same psychic science, a science using a different level of psychic equipment. All these sciences are the application of knowledge and thought at different levels. All relate to the fundamental principle that everything in the manifested universe is energy and that energy follows thought.

As I said, the sixth sub-race will develop the intuition, the knowledge of the soul, which comes down through the brain into consciousness. The function of the lower mind is to rationalise, to discriminate. You know from experience; you make equations. The intuition is beyond thought. It is the function of the soul before it has come down to the thought level. The soul knows on its own plane, and through the nervous system can make known that which it knows. You know without having to think.

So the sixth sub-race will become adept in the use of the intuition and this will be a big step forward for humanity.

Q. Is by any chance the flag of Britain, the Union Jack, an emblem of unity in diversity? (March 2007)

A. The Union Jack is an emblem of unity in diversity. That is exactly what it is. It represents the flags of England, Scotland, Northern Ireland and Wales.

Q. Why do the Russians seem to choose order over law and order, or order and control over real democracy? It appears that the electorate prefers a 'strong man' who will ensure security – although it might lead to more internal or external conflict. (April 2008)

A. With respect, this seems to me to be a rather simplistic analysis of the Russian situation. No country in the world has 'real democracy'. The Scandinavian countries are probably the closest to the ideal. The USA is run by, and for the benefit of, big business and the Pentagon; Britain and other European countries by ancient aristocratic power and big business.

Russia, like many countries, is in a state of transition. A look at the rays of Russia might shed light on its problems. The soul Ray is 7, the ray of ceremonial order or ritual or organisation, and this is potently moving this great country towards an organised unity and beneficent order. At the same time, the personality is 6, (the ray of idealism or devotion, and of the past age), expressed by the masses of its huge population. These two rays are moving and working in opposite directions and so engender an inevitable struggle. The people of Russia are profoundly religious. The Master Djwhal Khul (through Alice Bailey) has predicted that the new 7th-ray religion will emerge out of Russia.

DIVERSITY IN POLITICAL FORMS

POLITICAL FORMS IN THE NEW AGE

by the Master —, through Benjamin Creme

Present day political structures are of three main types, reflecting, however imperfectly, three separate aspects of the Divine intention. To these three forms we give the names of Democracy, Communism and Fascism. However distortedly, each embodies a divine idea; however corruptly, each is the expression of a divine energy, and each is related to a major planetary centre.

That which we call Democracy is a reflection, albeit inadequate today, of the love nature of God, exemplified by the Spiritual Hierarchy, the centre where the Love of God is expressed. That to which we give the name of Communism is an expression, as yet imperfect, of the Intelligence of God, centred in humanity itself; while Fascism, today in a totally distorted manner, reflects the energy of Will from Shamballa, the centre where the Will of God is known.

Each of these three forms of organisation and relationship is in a state of transition, more or less, and in their gradual transformation into a fuller expression of the divine idea behind them lies the hope of future peaceful co-operation.

Each of these forms today is characterised by a spirit of intense rivalry and exclusiveness. The followers of each are convinced that they alone have the answers to man's need for structure and organisation and are ready, if need be, to plunge the world into catastrophic war to uphold their particular system.

What of the future? How can we ensure that these apparently disparate and opposing modes of political thought do not overwhelm humanity? Very little foresight is needed to see that without a change of direction mankind faces

51

terrible dangers. There is no need to elaborate; the nuclear threat is clear to all.

An immediate first step is the realisation that humanity is One; its needs are the same, everywhere, however varied and apparently conflicting the outer forms. The enormous discrepancies in living standards between the rich and poor countries make mockery of this essential Oneness, and have within them the seeds of war.

The answer therefore is simple: the implementation of the principle of sharing provides the solution to the divisions in our planetary life. Nothing less will do. Sharing is divine, part of God's Plan for His children, and must one day become manifest.

And when men share, the divisions will grow together, the separations will be healed; and through the three major political structures the Love, the Will and the Intelligence of God will find a truer reflection. A true Democracy in which all men participate will take the place of the present sham. A new spirit of freedom will invest the Communist ideal with warmth and love. A truly spiritual hierarchy embodying the beneficent Will of God will one day replace the present authoritarian regimes.

Thus will it be. Thus will the outer forms reflect the inner divine life and purpose and so present to men new modes of expression and relationship through which their growing sense of the nature of God can be realised.

All awaits the acceptance of sharing – the key to justice and peace.

(*Share International*, December 1982)

DIVERSITY IN POLITICAL FORMS

Q. It is difficult for me to imagine how fascism could evolve into a more divinely inspired form of government. Can you talk about what fascism would look like in a more perfected form? (2) Would there be, for instance, a single leader directly inspired by the Spiritual Hierarchy?
A. (1) The country as a whole would be structured so as to express the highest, divine aspect of Will, so as to reflect the Hierarchical purpose. The political system would be hierarchical but would leave every citizen with complete freedom and social justice. (2) Yes there would be such a leader.

Q. I find it difficult to see how fascism, even in a purer form, can ever be seen as an attribute of divinity. Could you please explain further.
A. Fascism is related to the first ray aspect of Will or Purpose, centred in Shamballa where the will of God is known. This has nothing to do with the destructive totalitarianism of fascism today.

Q. Would a benevolent dictatorship such as Fidel Castro's in Cuba (at least in the early days) be considered 'fascism', reflecting, though quite imperfectly, the Will aspect of Shamballa?
A. No. Fidel Castro was trying to create communism in Cuba.

Q. At present, in 2012, which countries are potentially moving toward the fascistic political system?
A. China.

Q. The article by your Master, 'Political forms in the New Age', made me realise how wrong it is for the US to try to export or even force a democratic political system onto other

nations. (1) Is each nation destined to establish one of three political systems? (2) Will it be related to the composition of its population?
A. (1) Yes. Essentially but not in fact every nation is destined. (2) Yes.

Q. (1) Can the soul of a nation express better through a particular political system? (2) Is a nation's ray structure indicative of which political system takes root in that nation?
A. (1) Yes. (2) Yes.

Q. How do the three political forms the Master speaks about relate to the three Hierarchical experiments for the race?
A. The three political forms express the qualities of the Rays 1, 2 and 3, the Rays of Aspect: communism comes under the aegis of the 3rd Ray (Intelligence aspect and centered in humanity itself), democracy under the 2nd Ray (Love aspect centered in the Spiritual Hierarchy) and fascism under the 1st Ray (Will and Purpose aspect centered in Shamballa) – all in their perfected forms. The soul of a nation or individual when on the Rays of Attribute (rays 4, 5, 6 or 7) eventually has to find its correspondence on one of the three Rays of Aspect.

Q. You said the ideal ratio within an economic system for a stable nation is 70 per cent socialism and 30 per cent capitalism. Can they be established in any of these political forms or will it be different?
A. This ratio can be established in any of these three political forms.

Q. Do Presidents Castro, Chavez and Morales have a different form of government to Western democracy? (March 2007)
A. Fidel Castro, the last of the old-style Communist leaders, has run Cuba for these last approximately 50 years. To my

mind, he is somewhat out of date. Hugo Chavez is somewhat different and Evo Morales is different again.

Mr Chavez, who is an unconventional type of president, to say the least, has bright ideas. Some of them may be a little bit unusual but they are along a certain line. He comes out of the developing world. Venezuela was a very poor country until the discovery of its oil. Now it is a rich country with a huge oil reserve, and so suddenly has become important, especially to the United States. America does not like the tone of the Chavez government. It is too much to the left for those in power in America to contemplate having on their doorstep. It is too much like the Allende government in Chile, which the CIA got rid of. So the Americans give millions of dollars to boost the opposition forces in Venezuela, to bring as much pressure as they can against the Chavez government and try to undermine it in that way. There are many rich right-wing groups, businessmen in Venezuela, who are glad to have these millions of dollars for their propaganda and pressure groups to counter what seems to them the revolutionary force of the Chavez government. Meanwhile, Chavez himself is making a journey around the world and building contacts with many governments.

In Britain, our so-called New Labour party means a tiny per cent of Labour ideals and fair play, and a large amount, maybe 80 per cent, of commercialisation based on market forces. Maitreya says those governments in the world who blindly follow market forces are leading their people to destruction. And that is exactly what is happening all over the world.

Market forces by their very nature are killing off our civilisation. You can observe this destructive principle, commercialisation, driving all that is sane, all that is just, all that is even common sense, out of the economic process in the world. It is finding its way to turn every government agency such as health and education, and human beings themselves, into pawns of market forces.

Chavez and Morales do have slightly different forms of government but there are many forms. Some are called democratic, some semi-democratic, some are outstandingly undemocratic and so on. In time the world will become unified. The energies of Aquarius will inevitably bring about a greater synthesis, but today the energies of Pisces are driving people in different directions.

Q. Do you mean the world will become unified under one economic-political system? (March 2007)

A. The world could become unified in the American way, following the American economic system aligned with market forces based on competition. It serves a few well and the majority badly, and so creates the very schisms and anxieties, and eventually terrorism and war, that we have today. You might think that we could try to make the world one, in the sense of an American-style empire, a Pax Americana. Everyone would have the American idea of democracy, and somehow or other the world would go on greedily competing, without going to war. But this is a fantasy. It will never happen.

That is why we have war and terrorism today because the American view is of the past. And the world has been forced by its economic domination into forms of government and relationships that are intrinsically impossible for the future. The competition involved does not bring goodwill because it relates only to the past and has nothing to give to the future.

Goodwill is certainly what we need, but competition does not bring goodwill; it is the very opposite. It breeds what you would imagine, fighting over markets and driving hard bargains against one's competitors. That way leads to confrontation, and eventually war and more wars. It is the way of the past.

It is really a choice between competition and co-operation. Co-operation is the way of the future, and the only way that will serve humanity.

Q. Why is it that governments seem to be so ineffectual now? (March 2007)

A. The governments only know how to act in terms of the past, and these no longer apply. That is why there is no government on Earth today who can actually govern. They do their best, and all fail because fundamentally they are using outworn methods. Only one thing – the last thing to occur to them – will break the present impasse to which they have all come, and that is to inaugurate the system of sharing.

As soon as they do that they will create the trust that will enable them to tackle all other problems co-operatively. They have to be solved co-operatively. You cannot impose solutions on nations who do not want them. It can only happen by co-operation, when the trust generated by sharing is there and allows the change to take place. Then the goodwill engendered by trust will make possible the solution of problems which today seem impossible to solve.

Q. What do you think about Hugo Chavez and the rising tide of the left-wing governments in Latin America? Is that the shape of things to come in the world, with politicians working to eradicate poverty more and pandering to the rich less? (January/February 2007)

A. For anyone who wants to see justice and the end of poverty and hunger the answer to the question has to be 'Yes'. Chavez is trying to help his people out of endless, traditional, poverty and suffering, using oil money to do it – and, at the same time, fend off the attempts of the US to undermine his work. Hierarchy hold the view that the ideal relationship for sound social cohesion and justice is 70 per cent socialism and 30 per cent capitalism.

Q. Hugo Chavez has done much to serve his country so far, but he seems lately to have 'lost his balance' as evidenced in his attempts to change the constitution to allow him to hold office indefinitely. Your comments please. (October 2007)

A. There seems to be a misunderstanding. His programme of change is likely to take years to mature and he has many enemies at home and abroad, especially in the US administration. It is obvious, therefore, that he needs more time to carry out the reforms but that does not necessarily mean indefinitely.

Q. Recently Lebanon has seen the assassination of Rafik Hariri, Samir Kassir, George Hawi and Gebran Tueni, and the attempted assassination of Mai Chidaic and Elias Murr. Do you believe that the CIA was involved directly or indirectly with all of these incidents? If so, what do they hope to gain? (January/February 2006)

A. Not in all of them but in the assassination of Rafik Hariri and Gebran Tueni, and the attempted assassination of Mai Chidaic and Elias Murr. They will seek, as they have done in the killing of Rafik Hariri, to put the blame for these killings and attempted killings on the Syrians. All of this is part of the pressure being exerted on Syria to 'toe the line' in relation to helping the 'insurgency in Iraq'. To the US, Syria is one of the 'Triangle of Evil' with Iran and North Korea.

Q. What can humanity do to stop the rise of terrorism and destruction? (October 2010)

A. Terrorism, according to the Masters, is basically the result of injustice. There are other factors but the fundamental cause is a sense of injustice. There is no doubt at all that the G8 nations have usurped the goods and resources of the world for years and years. We have lived off the backs of people in the developing countries for countless years. The people in the developing nations naturally feel aggrieved and want to rectify this situation. They feel helpless; they do not know how to do it. One of the ways, the most aggressive way to do this, is to become a terrorist.

Terrorism is a terrible thing. It is a canker, but it is understandable if you know the cause. We need to seek the cause behind any act of aggression: what is the cause behind war, behind terrorism? You will find that the cause of terrorism is a deep sense of grievance, a sense of being given only a particle of life. Terrorists feel that they have only a fragment of what the rich and powerful nations like America, European countries and Japan have. It does not feel fair. They are human beings who feel they are part of humanity – which they are – and yet they are not given a chance to live at their best, to give their utmost to life. And so, many of them, often the youngest and bravest, turn to terrorism.

To think that you can wage a war against terrorism is a nonsense. You can fight a war against a country but you cannot make war against an unknown enemy. You cannot fight against terrorism. It is fluid and does not exist as a nation. There are probably terrorists in every country without exception. There are terrorists in the USA who come from various countries and are against America. There are also terrorists in America who are born and bred American, and are deeply hurt and disgusted by some aspects of life in the USA.

This cannot go on. This country, the USA, makes enemies wherever it goes. It is as if America cannot exist without an enemy. You have to have an enemy. Why? To prove you are big and strong? We know you are big and strong. America is like a big, strong, healthy youth: brash and conscious of his muscles and that he is invincible. He is rather aggressive and vaunts his youth and power. America is very young as a nation. Grow up; give yourselves time to grow up; stop vaunting your muscles, your strength and your weaponry by making enemies out of this country and that.

America has made more wars against others, since the end of the Second World War, than any other country. Make your government stop war. You are the ones who will do it. You are the ones who can make your government obey the law of life. The law of life is the very opposite of that which allows war. We have to put war out of our consciousness altogether. Nothing is solved by war. War simply makes for more war and more grieving, more discord and, today, terrorism of all kinds.

Terrorism is becoming more and more sophisticated. You cannot fight it by war because you do not know where it is coming from. It could come out of any country in the world.

Q. Do you have any information about the future of Cuba when Fidel Castro goes? (May 2007)

A. Cuba has been an artificial state for a long time, the result of two forms of action, one mainly from Fidel Castro himself and one from the United States government. The United States government has withheld any aid or even trade with Cuba for years. At the same time Castro – and he has some very fine qualities – has been a long-term dictator in Cuba, and a dictatorship of any kind, beneficent or otherwise, is no good to anybody. So the people of Cuba could advance very quickly if America stopped its embargo and if Castro retired and gave up control of every aspect of Cuban life.

Dictatorship, even beneficent dictatorship, is no answer to the needs of humanity. People have to be free. And that freedom has to be in relation to a sense of justice. In Cuba there is a degree of justice but no political freedom. Justice and freedom are intertwined. Both are divine, both necessary for the divinity of every human being.

The end of Castro's reign will really be a good thing for the Cuban people in the long term. They will grow into themselves, think for themselves and have freedom and justice together.

Q. If the US and other forces were to ask for advice from Hierarchy, what advice and solutions to the terrible mess of Afghanistan and Iraq would they receive? (October 2007)

A. To admit the wrong committed by the invasions and to pour the necessary monies and all other resources to restore these countries to peace and calm. To hold an international UN-led inquiry into the best way to begin and complete this restoration and to avow no further incursions of a like kind anywhere in the world.

Q. (1) Are coalition governments the way forward for many political systems that suffer from oppositional conflictual party politics? (2) Is it a form of consensus government which we may see more of in future? (May 2010)
A. (1) Yes. (2) Yes.

Q. What will it take to convince both sides in the Palestinian-Israeli conflict that they must negotiate to arrive at a point where peace and tolerance become possible? (January/February 2009)
A. It is easy to say they should negotiate but the gap between the two sides is very wide and I am convinced that it will take Maitreya to bring them together. The problem is that a negotiated peace has to be fair to last. So far, the Palestinians have never been offered a fair or just solution. Nor has Israel been open to negotiation on crucial matters of difference.

I believe that a worldwide embargo of Israel, such as was applied to South Africa, and led to the end of apartheid, would be the most effective way to bring Israel to the negotiating table.

Q. Is boycotting the products of a country – for example, Israel – really effective? Do boycotts not always harm the poorer people in a country? (October 2011)
A. It depends on the country. Boycotting is a way for the international community to demonstrate its disapproval of unlawful practices. It is rather a blunt instrument and, depending on the kind of boycott, can affect rich or poor or all citizens of the boycotted countries.

Q. If the action Israel took in 1967 during the Six-day War constituted 'evil', are we seeing the same energy at work with regard to their actions against the Palestinians, particularly those in the Gaza strip? (January/February 2009)

A. Yes.

Q. In June 2010 Israeli armed forces boarded a flotilla that had roughly 700 pro-Palestinian activists on board. About nine activists were killed, many were placed under arrest and the rest are being deported. (1) Was this an act of evil due to Israel's government being influenced by the remnants of the Antichrist energies, what you refer to as "nefarious energies", which were defeated during WWII? (2) Is this also the result of the fact, according to your information, that many in the Israeli government and military were German military officers in their past lives and supporters of Nazi ideology? (3) Some commentators have suggested that Israel could have let the boat land and arrested the people at that time as opposed to boarding the vessel at sea. Did Israel choose to take the bellicose actions it did to send a message not to trifle with Israel? (July/August 2010)

A. (1) Yes. That is behind the determination of the Israeli government (in association with the Pentagon) to maintain the tension in the Middle East, thus increasing worldwide tension and stress. (2) Yes. (3) Yes.

Q. Israel's military power depends on American financing and supplies. Will the economic collapse in the US and around the globe have a positive impact on the conflict between Israel and Palestine? (January/February 2009)

A. Mr Obama has already said words to the effect that America would stand behind Israel but financial pressures may cause some lessening of US financial support. In any case, I am sure it will take Maitreya to reconcile these two groups.

Q. In the short term Maitreya will undoubtedly have to suggest a land-for-peace deal between the Israelis and Palestinians. However, in the long term will the nation of Israel cease to officially exist and become part of Palestine once again with no partition? (November 2010)

A. No, I do not think Israel will cease to exist – too much time has passed for that – but the two nations will live side by side, sharing the resources of the area together.

Q. At the end of July 2011 over 100,000 Israelis took to the streets to protest against social injustice and the cost of living in Israel. Could your Master comment on whether this is the beginning of an 'Israeli' spring and will it lead to a fairer society in Israel, as well as – eventually – in Palestine? (September 2011)

A. It is a start in the right direction.

Q. What is Israel's role in the new world order? (November 2010)

A. Israel's role in the new world order is to kneel down and pray for forgiveness for what it is doing to the Palestinians. Then get on with the reality of dividing the land of Palestine to make two solid and viable nations – Israel and Palestine. The future for Israel is penitence and the resurgence of the natural goodwill of its people and the overcoming of the evil that the government is creating in Palestinian lands.

Q. (1) Has Maitreya been asked about the situation between Israel and the Palestinians now that the blockade of Gaza has captured the world's attention? If so, (2) what is the general nature of His response? (July/August 2010)

A. (1) Yes. (2) Maitreya deplores the present tragic situation of the Palestinians and makes His viewpoint clear. He urges the USA, instead of supporting the cruel actions of the Israeli government, to use its influence with the Israelis to end this inhuman blockade and to begin negotiations for peace.

Q. Should the illegal Jewish settlements on the West Bank (and East Jerusalem) be evacuated to make a just peace treaty possible? (July/August 2011)
A. Yes.

Q. Some groups and organisations support the Palestinians' plea for a one-state solution in which all citizens, Jewish and Palestinian, have the same democratic rights in one country. How does Hierarchy see such a solution? (July/August 2011)
A. An excellent solution except that it is probably unattainable. Therefore, They favour a two-state solution.

*Q. **Share International** seems to give a lot of attention to problem areas in the world, like the Middle East and to issues such as Palestine and Israel. Why do you give so much print space to these stories?* (January/February 2006)
A. Because the resolution of the conflicts taking place there is essential for world peace.

Q. After the inspiring events during the Orange Revolution last year some people now are disappointed about the President of Ukraine, Viktor Yuschenko. Could you provide your perspective on Ukraine? (January/February 2006)
A. There is all the difference in the world between leading and inspiring an idealistic grouping of people and implementing practically the hopes and ideals of these people. In office, Mr Yuschenko is finding it far harder to fulfil the hopes of so many. They should not rely on one, not very practical, man. They need to elect a team of practical idealists and work together for the good of all.

Q. Maitreya has said that we are our "brother's keeper". Does this apply on an international scale? For example, should the rest of the world stand by while a country like Zimbabwe spirals even further out of control into devastating chaos? Some call for the Zimbabwean people to rise up and overthrow the corrupt leadership. The world expects African leaders to take action. Meanwhile the violence, misery and hunger escalate. (July/August 2008)

A. The United Nations should be invited by the African leaders to investigate thoroughly and act if necessary.

Q. Neighbouring countries are often at war, and within countries (as in many parts of Africa) there is conflict between peoples, tribes, ethnic and religious groups. The culprit is said to be the former colonial masters who deliberately established national boundaries in a divide-and-rule policy. Was it not more a case of ignorance and insensitivity rather than a deliberate act of dividing up peoples and tribes that had traditional, cultural and/or ethnic ties? (October 2007)

A. Yes, I believe it is more the result of ignorance and insensitivity than deliberate policy.

Q. It is hard to imagine what the world would have been like without colonialism. (1) Was it 'part of the Plan'? (2) Was colonialism more beneficial or more negative in its effect, speaking in very general terms? (October 2007)

A. (1) No. (2) The effects of colonialism are varied, often depending on the approach, habits and methods of the colonising power. In very general terms, despite having caused much unhappiness, colonialism has brought more benefits to humanity than otherwise.

Q. Corruption in developing countries often puts off would-be donors. While the monitoring of corruption and transparency levels is welcome, the definition of corruption leads to results skewed against developing countries where corruption is generally individual and also in reaction to the world's unfair economic and trade systems. Large-scale governmental, military, multinational and political corruption in industrialised countries tends to be overlooked in such monitoring. Would it be accurate to say that large, rich and powerful countries contribute to corruption in poorer countries and in what way? (October 2007)

A. That is not the question. Corruption is worldwide, greater by far in effect in the developed countries, because of the enormous amounts of money involved, than in the poorer areas of the world. Furthermore, the corruption that does exist in the developing world is not only more noticeable but gives the developed world's governments an easy excuse not to send aid to these 'corrupt' governments.

ELECTIONS

Q. How fair were the recent US elections (November 2006), which saw the Democratic Party return to power in Congress?

A. About 35 per cent were fair, which means that had they been nearer 100 per cent fair it would have been a landslide victory for the Democrats. (December 2006)

Q. Were the electronic voting machines tampered with, as in the 2004 US elections, to give advantage to the Republicans, but just not enough for them to win? (December 2006)

A. Some of them, yes, but less than in the previous election. The other methods, intimidation, etc, were well in evidence.

Q. Does President George W. Bush know of the full corruption in his country's voting system? (December 2006)

A. No. He leaves these details to his staff.

Q. Who won the election in Mexico? (November 2006)

A. Strangely enough, it was an almost completely free and fair election, unlike the last two elections in the United States – the last one being the most corrupt, I think, that has ever taken place in a modern state.

You must make sure that you do not have another election like that. Do not stand for it. The voting machines were pre-programmed to change every fifth vote for Kerry into one for Bush. Those elections were completely false. Ohio was actually won by Kerry, although he lost it. Florida was won by Kerry, so was New Mexico. The result would have been completely different but for the corruption. There was a massive vote against Bush but also a strong vote for him. But Kerry won the election and was denied it, just as in the previous election Al Gore won the election and was denied it. The world would be a completely different place had either Gore or Kerry become President. We might have had Maitreya out in the open now.

Q. Did vote tampering take place in the recent (2008) US presidential elections? (December 2008)

A. Yes, but to a lesser degree than the last two elections.

Q. If so, what would the real results have been – without vote rigging and other tricks? (December 2008)

A. About 5 per cent higher for Barack Obama.

Q. What is your opinion about the recent elections in Iran such as the electoral process and the alleged results? (1) How accurate were the stated results? (2) Which president would have been better for Iran in the long run: Ahmadinejad or Mousavi? (July/August 2009)

67

A. (1) I believe that the Iranian elections, like ex-President Bush's two elections, were deeply flawed by serious 'rigging' by the incumbent party. The public reaction in Tehran can be well understood and justified. (2) Mr Mousavi.

Q. The International Atomic Energy Agency has recently reported that Iran is attempting to develop nuclear weapons. Do you think this report is accurate, and if so, what if anything should the world community do about this? (December 2011)

A. My information is that this growing assumption by America, Israel and other states, is not accurate. My information is that Iran is focusing its nuclear programme, as it says, for peaceful purposes only, but that they want to develop a system where they would, if attacked, have the possibility of creating a retaliatory weapon. They want it both ways – in other words they're not creating weapons of assault but want to have the possibility of retaliation if attacked. One should not forget that Israel has nuclear weapons.

Q. (1) In the French Presidential elections, voting machines were introduced for the first time in France, on the initiative of the Minister of the Interior, Mr Sarkozy. Was there any fraud in the elections? (2) With the election of Mr Sarkozy, do the Hierarchy foresee forthcoming social unrests in France? (June 2007)

A. (1) Yes, but a small percentage compared with some recent elections elsewhere. (2) Not particularly.

Q. More and more elections seem to be contested in various parts of the world. (1) Is this an indication that many elections are rigged? (2) Is it also indicative of the failure of politics as we know it to answer people's real needs? (3)

Has adverserial-style party politics had its day? (January/February 2008)

A. (1) Yes, and in major countries that take the greatest exception to 'rigging' in developing nations. (2) Yes. (3) Yes. The people want to see their needs being met above all.

Q. Was the 2007 Kenyan election rigged? (January/February 2008)

A. Yes, to some extent.

Q. Does the election of Barack Obama mean that the soul aspect of America can more easily manifest itself? (December 2008)

A. Not necessarily. He has not done anything yet! A better indication will come when the US public hear and assess Maitreya. The African-American community will feel empowered and vindicated by Barack Obama's election victory but almost half of the popular vote, 48 per cent, went to the Republicans. The breakdown of America's economic and financial hegemony will be very influential in the months ahead.

Q. Much, perhaps too much, is expected of the new American President. Do you think the world is being too optimistic? Barack Obama is expected to solve the major current world crises: the economic crisis, the environment, unemployment, collapsing industries, growing homelessness, rising poverty, conflict in the Middle East and terrorism. Surely such a task would take a superman to get to grips with? (January/February 2009)

A. Absolutely true. Luckily, we do have a superman who really can show us the way to solve these problems – His name is Maitreya. The rest is up to us. We have to make the right decisions in the light of Maitreya's ideas. Obama could be a decisive voice for a 'new' America – co-operative and willing to listen to others – in the world.

Q. The elections and the prospect of a new era in US politics with Barack Obama as President seems to have lifted the spirits of Americans and many others around the world. Do you expect a new phase of moderation and negotiation instead of warmongering? (January/February 2009)

A. Yes. He probably would not immediately withdraw from Iraq or Afghanistan, but as soon as possible, whatever that means. We can look forward to dealing with a President who does not seem to speak or act from ideological demagogy, who is empirical and moderate and who has a very sick country to restore to health. He has this in his favour – Maitreya and His vision, energy and love. What an example for him to follow!

Q. Are there any politicians in Japan who are inspired by Maitreya? (September 2010)

A. There are those who have heard of Maitreya and His priorities and who think highly of this information but who do not act because they feel helpless. There are a few who are what you would call directly inspired – but by the Master in Tokyo. The Master in Tokyo has disciples through whom He works. In every country are being gathered people who are responsive to the wider world rather than to their own individual country. These people will provide the frameworks of the new governments that will be formed, by democratic election, in every country. Sincerity and altruism will be the hallmarks of the new governments.

Q. Are there politicians in the world who are inspired by Maitreya? (September 2010)

A. There are very few politicians of the old school who know or care anything about Maitreya. But in the centres, especially in those where a Master lives [London, New York,

70

Tokyo, Darjeeling, Geneva, Moscow, Rome], there are a growing number of selected groups of people who have been brought together. They know the Plan and know what humanity needs, and through their obvious lack of ego and obvious sincerity they will be put in positions of influence and power.

These questions are often about individuals. The energies of Aquarius, however, only work through groups. The idea of an enlightened or strong person coming out and forming a group is changing. But when a group is working as a group, not as individuals, then the energies of Aquarius can be contacted and used.

Q. It is becoming clearer every day that politicians do not know what to do and have no answers to the growing world crisis. Are there any politicians or leaders in the world at present who have any inkling of how to proceed and how to tackle the growing problems? (November 2011)

A. Yes, but they are not yet in office.

AMERICAN CONSPIRACIES

Q. Why would the man who is posing as Saddam Hussein go on so long with the lie? He is putting himself through much grief, for what? (December 2006)

A. The outrageous and sinister truth is that the poor man who has just been sentenced to hanging no longer realises that he is not Saddam Hussein but a look-alike cousin. For a year, in the hands of the CIA, he has been systematically brainwashed by chemicals and hypnosis to forget his own identity and assume that of Saddam Hussein, President of Iraq.

These methods have been used by many of the intelligence agencies in the world for very many years, especially for transforming and using captured spies. It was for this process to be carried out that this stand-in for Saddam Hussein disappeared from public view, after his capture, for so long.

Q. Will the world ever find out the truth about the 'wrong' Saddam Hussein being executed? (January/February 2007)

A. Yes, I believe it will. I think that Maitreya, Himself, will bring the subject up, or, if not, someone is bound to ask Him relevant questions about it.

Q. Where is the body of the real Saddam Hussein? (January/February 2007)

A. It is buried in Tikrit, in the north of Iraq, which is the tribal home of Saddam Hussein.

Q. How much DNA is shared by cousins? (January/February 2007)

A. It varies, of course, but about 75 per cent. The only DNA the US authorities had to compare the stand-in Saddam with was Saddam Hussein's sons'. So the DNA evidence claimed as proof of Saddam Hussein's identity is false.

Q. On 26 March 2010, a South Korean warship was sunk close to the North-South Korean maritime border. The South Korean investigation into the cause of the sinking has concluded that a torpedo fired from a North Korean submarine was to blame. The US and other governments have condemned North Korea, but the North claims that so-called evidence was deliberately planted and strongly denies any involvement. Did a North Korean submarine really fire the torpedo? (June 2010)

A. My information is that North Korea had nothing to do with the sinking of the South Korean ship. My information is that the true culprit is the American CIA, to bring further pressure on North Korea.

Q. Recently I saw the G20 on television where the US President and South Korean President were hugging each other and smiling. I wondered if the President of South Korea knew their warship had been sunk by the American CIA (see **Share International** *June 2010). South Korea and the US are alliance partners. I can't believe he could greet the US President pleasantly if he knew what had been done by the CIA.*

(1) Does he know the crime was done by the CIA? (2) Does the US President know the true culprit is the American CIA and kept silent to avoid anticipated troubles? (3) Did the US President have the CIA sink the South Korean ship? (4) Did the CIA take action independently? (5) If so, it indicates the CIA is not under control. Isn't it a menace to the world? (6) Is there any other country who knows the true culprit? (7) If the US President knows the true culprit, shouldn't he sincerely ask for forgiveness about the murder and the planned false charge to South Korea and North Korea? (January/February 2011)

A. (1) No. (2) No. (3) No. (4) Yes. (5) Yes. (6) Probably not. (7) Yes, but he does not know.

Q. The killing of Osama bin Laden by an American special attack force in Pakistan has just been announced. He is said to have been shot in the eye and killed (though unarmed) and the body to have been buried at sea, that is, not retrievable for inspection. Can you say if this is indeed the end of Bin Laden? (June 2011)

A. I do believe that Osama bin Laden is no longer alive, but this report from the US administration does not tally with my information, which is that Osama bin Laden died peacefully, after a long struggle with illness, in 2006. Before he died he wished to maintain his call for 'justice' (as he understood the term) and arranged for one of his many younger brothers to maintain the myth of his presence.

Q. In 2007 Benazir Bhutto (former Prime Minister of Pakistan who was assassinated) said in an interview that Osama bin Laden was dead. (1) Was she right? (2) How did he die? (3) Where is his body buried? (4) If this scenario is accurate, why was his death kept secret? (5) Supposing these are the facts, how long have the Americans known of Osama bin Laden's demise? (June 2011)

A. (1) Yes. (2) He died after a long struggle with cancer and kidney disease. (3) It was not buried but burned. (4) He wanted to maintain the myth as a rallying call for the young. (5) They probably believed he was still alive. (June 2011)

Q. Why was Osama bin Laden shot? Why was he not captured and brought to justice? (June 2011)

A. Ask the Americans.

Q. Why was his body "buried at sea"? (June 2011)

A. Ask the Americans.

Q. There is something very fishy about the reports of how Osama bin Laden died. It is reminiscent of the feel of the so-called accounts of how Saddam Hussein was 'found' and other 'facts' around his 'trial' and so on. Your comments, please. (June 2011)

A. Quite so.

Q. One of the news reports showing the compound where Osama bin Laden was shot mentioned that there was no sign of a kidney dialysis machine, yet it was well-known that Bin Laden had serious kidney problems. Does the absence of a dialysis machine not point to the possibility that Osama bin Laden had not been living at the compound? (June 2011)

A. My information is that he never lived at that compound.

THE UNITED NATIONS

Q. Is a so-called 'World Government' ever likely to come into existence? (November 2010)

A. No. Hierarchy's plans do not include the formation of a one world government. Rather, the United Nations is seen as the platform for all international problems to be brought forward and talked through. Each nation is seen as having its own destiny and its own rays or energy structure, which bring about that destiny and give quality to the individuality of each. One could say in a phrase, that 'unity in diversity' is nearer the vision of Hierarchy.

Q. Would you comment on the apparent paradox between your position supporting the future role of the United Nations in world politics and the concept of free will. (June 2011)

A. I do not see any contradiction at all. The UN is not a world government but a 'sounding board' for the exchange of all different, perhaps contradictory, ideas, and is essential to the free exchange of such ideas. It is the hope of humanity for a better and better ordered, peaceful, humane world.

Q. You have said that some problems will only be solved after Maitreya's emergence. Is this also true of the reforming of the United Nations? (March 2007)

A. The United Nations is not in the mood yet for the extraordinary reform of getting rid of the veto. There is no way at the moment that America is going to give up the use of the veto, and I would say the same for Britain, France,

Russia and China. They all love that veto and the power it gives them.

So as far as United Nations reconstruction is concerned, I do not think anything like that would happen until Maitreya is well and truly established, and His views are made known. There is no way that the United Nations would reach a truly democratic existence while pressure from the Security Council and the veto persists, and the democratic voice of the General Assembly is not heard. I cannot see that happening until Maitreya is accepted, and His thoughts, ideas and priorities are guiding humanity. I think it will take Maitreya to bring that about.

SHARING

THE CASE FOR SHARING

by the Master —, through Benjamin Creme

There will shortly come a time when humanity must reach a great decision. Troubled as it is on all sides by divisions and cleavage, a new approach must be found to the many problems which beset it. Without such a new approach, there is little doubt, an ominous future would await mankind.

Historically, there is no precedent for the present situation and conditions on Earth. Never before have so many souls co-existed on the planet. Seldom, if ever, have the divisions between the groups been so painful and deep. Never has man controlled such forces of destruction as are now at his command, giving him power to destroy the life in every kingdom. When such destruction threatens, man must take stock and devise new ways to proceed.

Of all the possible ways there yet remains but one untried. Throughout his history one simple answer has eluded man's grasp. The principle of Sharing is the only one which will answer man's needs and solve his many problems, for it is fundamental to the Plan of God Himself. Without sharing, man denies his divinity and stores up for himself all future woes. Without sharing, unholy chaos reigns and withholds from man the Justice which is his by right. Sharing alone provides the opportunity to establish God's Plan of Brotherhood and to remove from the world for ever the sin of separation.

How, lacking sharing, could man continue? How, without sharing, could he hope to survive? So great are the dangers in the present imbalance between the nations that luck alone would not suffice to see him through. A deadly sickness – separation and greed – prevails upon the Earth, and calls for drastic measures to effect a cure.

The simple cure is at hand despite the outer chaos. The long-drawn testing of mankind is all but at an end. Arrayed against the forces which still hold man in thrall, the Hierarchy of Light retrace Their steps and stand together under the banner of Truth.

Maitreya's mission begins with an appeal to men to share. His knowledge of men's hearts leaves Him certain of their choice, and certain of their readiness to make the needed changes. "Man must share or die," has He said, knowing well that men will choose to share and live and to create with Him a better future.

Until now, all efforts to solve man's problems have been directed to maintaining the present structures, however unjust they have proved themselves to be. The cleavages on every hand cry out for resolution and await the application of the Law of Justice.

Fear grips many today as they hear their leaders wrangle; a time is coming when they will leave their leaders far behind. Man is awakening to the call for freedom and needs only true leadership to set the world to rights. Maitreya has come to show the way and to lead men to brotherhood and justice. A new era opens under His wise direction which will demonstrate the true divinity of man, establishing the means of sharing and co-operation and thus fulfilling the Plan of God.

(*Share International*, March 1987)

SHARING – THE ONLY WAY FOR PEACE

Q. Would you kindly outline the practical steps nations could take to implement global sharing? (April 2008)

A. There is a group of Masters already in the world, 14 Masters and Maitreya. Their disciples have created a series of alternative, interrelated plans, blueprints which if implemented would solve the redistribution problems at the heart of the economic problem today. The resources are there. There is more food in the world than we need, much of it rotting away in the storehouses of the developed world while millions die of hunger elsewhere. These interrelated plans outline a very simple method of redistribution.

There are various plans, but this one is the simplest and best. Humanity might or might not adopt it, but some variation of this might be acceptable. First of all, each nation would be asked to make known what they make, what they grow, what they import. In this way the total goods of the Earth would be known. Each nation would be asked to donate to a central pool that which it has in excess of its needs.

The rich and powerful nations, obviously, would put in more because they have so much excess. The poorer nations would put in less because they have less, but all would put in what they have in excess of what they need. Out of that central pool, created by all the nations, the needs of all would be met. This is taking into account the needs of the planet.

We ruin and ravage the planet. It is abused and is now sick. This plan of redistribution would take into account what we have to do, for example, in a world that is becoming more and more denuded of trees. We must plant more trees, never use beyond a certain number. We get our oxygen from the vegetable kingdom, and at the same time the vegetable kingdom is a wonderful absorber of carbon dioxide. So the more trees we destroy the less oxygen we have and the more 'carbon footprints' we make. Eighty per cent of global warming is created by misguided humanity itself.

Then there are those like the American President [George W. Bush] who declares that there is no global warming. "It does not exist," he says. This, in a country that produces 25 per cent of the world's pollution! One country produces a quarter of the world's pollution and denies its effect.

Q. Sharing is an admirable aim and also what is needed in the world, but it is the one thing that people are least likely to do. Just take a look around. Even otherwise 'good' people just don't seem to be willing to do that. Selfishness, it seems to me, is pandemic. I wonder what on earth has to happen to change this mindset. Being willing to share is very different to being forced to share. What does Maitreya have up his sleeve to change the mindset of 6 billion people, other than the Day of Declaration experiences, which I don't think will be enough to do it, as many will put it down to fraud, hallucination, etc? (May 2008)

A. This is a quite common reaction to my information, even by people who have no difficulty in accepting the fact of the Masters or Maitreya, or the urgent need for sharing as the only way to justice and peace. However, I believe it is profoundly mistaken. It is true that we have fallen into a deep materiality which demonstrates as the stranglehold that commercialisation now has on every aspect of our lives. Commercialisation, Maitreya warns, is more dangerous to humanity than an atomic bomb.

One of the problems is the difficulty the average person has in visualising the means by which sharing will come about. People tend to think of sharing in purely personal terms: they imagine being personally forced to share their income with strangers across the seas. The principle of sharing, when humanity sees the necessity, will be organised globally, each nation giving to a central pool only what it has in excess of its needs. From the common pool the needs of all will be met.

This will not happen unless and until humanity accepts the principle of sharing. Our free will is never infringed by the Masters. In reality, in the really real world (not the commercial world) we have no option but to share. Every other method has been tried and has failed and has led to the present sorry state of the world economic structure (which is teetering on a knife-edge) and which has brought the ecology of the planet to a dangerous imbalance. Sharing alone can establish the necessary trust between the nations required to tackle seriously the many dangerous problems facing humanity. What has Maitreya 'up His sleeve' to coax us to do the right and only thing to save our planet? His energy of Love, which goes right to the heart and brings out the best in men and women. No one knows the power of Maitreya.

Q. Commercialisation seems to be winning – if you look at Christmas shopping and New Year's fireworks around the world and all the spending on sales. Popular culture (so-called) looks like a vehicle for commercialisation. Your comments, please. (January/February 2007)

A. Commercialisation is not winning. It is, however, growing and reaching a climax of influence in every aspect of our lives. Because of market forces (which Maitreya calls the "forces of evil"), commercialisation has entered into everyone's life and Christmas is no exception to this trend. It will continue until we wake up and realise how the values of commerce are squeezing the sap out of every human act and reverence for life.

Sharing, we will eventually find, is the only answer to this growing alienation from the 'eternal verities'. Maitreya says that commercialisation is more dangerous than an atomic bomb.

Q. I'm aware of the importance of Maitreya's priorities but how can we apply them even in a new business? (June 2007)

A. Think what the essence of it is. The essence of Maitreya's priorities is the principle of sharing.

You can start the business as the boss, employ 20 people, pay them as little as possible, make them work for the longest hours for minimum pay. That is common today. This is called the effect of market forces. It drives the life out of life. Market forces turn people into automata, pawns moved around by people in power. It is happening all over the world. People see it but it is happening so quickly and subtly that they don't actually take it in. Why am I earning less per hour, working longer hours than I did 10 years ago? Why is my standard of living falling though that of the country as a whole is supposed to be going up?

So what do you do? You might start your new business as a co-operative. You employ 20 people, for example, and share the money you make. No one gets more than the others. Everyone works as hard as everyone else. You try to keep the hours you all work to a minimum and pay everyone the maximum for what they do. It is the New Age formula. When you begin to work in this way you understand what is meant by synthesis; that way you create groups. The energy of Aquarius only works in a synthetic way – through groups. It has no individual application.

You have to transform your whole idea of making money and becoming rich. If you do it the Aquarian way you're not going to become fantastically rich or you are all going to become rich.

Maitreya says the economy of a country is like a cart. It needs two wheels – capitalism and socialism. You need a combination of these two. From the Masters' point of view the best combination is 70 per cent socialism and 30 per cent capitalism. That is the best means for the greatest wellbeing of all the people in the country.

Q. (1) Now that the US Congress has passed a financial bailout plan, how close is the US and the world to the worldwide stock market crash that **Share International** *magazine has predicted? (2) Are we heading for a total economic collapse, or depression, worldwide, or (3) are the economic problems we are facing more limited in scope?* (November 2008)

A. (1) This is the crash. We could not be closer. (2) Not total perhaps, but very far-reaching. (3) No. The entire economic system and thinking must be transformed. It will take the adoption of the principle of sharing to bring that about.

Q. Will Maitreya's message of sharing be more difficult to accept for some people now, given that the economic situation of many millions in the US and other developed nations is increasingly precarious? (November 2008)

A. On the contrary, it will show these nations that the old greedy and selfish ways do not work in a rational manner. Only sharing, in the end, will bring stability, justice and the peace we all desire.

Q. The International Monetary Fund seems to be gaining a new level of importance as more and more economies begin to suffer from the economic collapse. What should or could best happen to the IMF? Is it also doomed to disappear along with other bodies that help maintain traditional capitalism? (December 2008)

A. The IMF is deeply disliked and distrusted, especially by the developing countries that have been driven to its door by desperation. Time after time countries have been given money, which they badly need, at the cost of their free will and the right to develop according to their traditions. They have been forced to grow food, for example, on a large scale for the foreign market and to buy their people's food from abroad. They are trapped. It is useful for countries at the moment who are suffering from the current economic crisis but eventually, when the principle of sharing reigns, it will be disbanded and close its doors. It has been blatantly a tool used for purely political ends.

Q. So many countries are beginning to suffer the fallout from the economic collapse. Vast amounts of money are promised to shore up crumbling industries and the financial sector, but surely it is the little people who are suffering even more than usual. What can the Masters do to help the already poverty-stricken and those now falling into debt, homelessness and unemployment? (January/February 2009)

A. It is not the Masters' place to solve our problems. We are responsible for the chaos. To directly interfere would be an infringement of our free will. During the 'good times' most people gave little thought to the poor and homeless. The Masters give the teaching that would rid the world of poverty and war at a stroke.

Q. Many people seem nervous about the economic health of their countries at present but there are still financiers promising that an upturn is just around the corner, that this is just a 'healthy adjustment'. People don't know how best to proceed – save, spend, invest or carry on as normal. Your comments, please. (January/February 2009)

A. As the Master says so clearly, this is not a temporary 'downturn' or 'healthy adjustment' we are all going through, but the collapse of the old, unjust order. It is necessary, and inevitable too, the logical outcome of our greed and selfishness. My advice, for what it is worth, is to save and learn to live more simply. This we all will have to do so that others may live at all.

Q. If all our savings and pension funds are going to go up in smoke, and if no one will be able to buy anything any more because of the current economic crisis, how can the world keep on running? (January/February 2009)

A. The outlook is not as bleak and extreme as you think. The basics will continue to be made and sold – and Maitreya will show a better, more just and fair way to live. You can see now why Maitreya has had to wait so long to speak publicly. Humanity, apart from the developing world, was living in illusion for years, thinking that a totally corrupt and unfair economic system could continue for ever. They forget about the ever-increasing effect of the energies of Aquarius.

Q. We hear a lot these days about "bail-out packages" to jump start nations' economies, as well as increased government spending on their countries' infrastructure in order to create jobs. Also, countries already have enormous amounts of national and foreign debt, and are printing money around the clock. Will all this make it even more difficult to switch to an economy based on sharing? Do not the debts have to be paid off first? (January/February 2009)

A. These money-spending policies will not work. This is not a Roosevelt New Deal. The times are very different although the present situation resembles that of the 1930s. This is the end of the Age, and order (or disorder) is not a passing storm. It will help people to see sharing as the only way to restructure the world economy.

Q. Why doesn't Maitreya appear under His real name in the television interviews? I think it would be better. (July/August 2010)

A. Sorry, but Maitreya does not agree with you. Many people want the world to change but they are passive. They want it to happen magically. They think of Maitreya as a big avatar and therefore think it is His job. It is not. It is our job. Long ago Maitreya said: "Every stone, every brick of the new civilisation must be put in place by humanity itself." More recently, He said: "I am the Architect, only, of the Plan.

You, My friends and brothers, are the willing builders of the Shining Temple of Truth."

He must know, and will know, that when people respond to His ideas, they want the changes in the world which He is advocating – not because of His status, not because He is the World Teacher. If a World Teacher says we need to share, it is easier to believe the Teacher than to see for oneself that sharing is the only possible answer to our problems.

When you see that sharing is the only way to justice and therefore to peace, you are making an inner spiritual step in awareness. Not everyone sees this. Why do you see this? Because you have this spiritual awareness. It is the result of an inner awareness. But if you just accept it because you have recognised Maitreya it doesn't mean that you are aware of the need. He has to know that enough people are responding from their own spiritual awareness.

Why do millions of people not share now? Why do people not see inwardly that sharing is a natural thing in a family of brothers? In a home the mother, father and children share everything. Likewise, we are in a home called Earth and we are brothers and sisters. Everything on Earth belongs to everyone and therefore should be shared. Everyone's needs should be met. But it is not happening, because people do not have that inner spiritual awareness. They do not make it happen. It does not occur to them.

We have free will. We can choose to share or not. If we decide to follow Maitreya's advice (whether we know it is His advice or not is immaterial) we will save the world. If we decide, however, that we do not want sharing, if there are not enough people who want change, sharing and justice, then we will destroy ourselves. It is as simple as that.

Maitreya knows that there is a 'critical mass' of 1.8 billion people ready to adopt His advocacy. When those 1.8 billion people make known where they stand and demand that their governments change their ways of working and share the resources of the world, it will happen.

Q. Maitreya has said that Britain will develop a model for an art of civilisation. What is Maitreya referring to? (May 2011)

A. A civilisation based on economic justice, political freedom and order.

Q. The Irish vote against the European Union calls into question its continued existence. Was the EU doomed from the start? Or could it be transformed into something more positive along the lines of the British Commonwealth model? How does the Hierarchy see the EU? (July/August 2008)

A. The EU was founded as an economic common market. It is not part of Hierarchy's Plan that the individual countries of Europe be 'lost' in a unified political State of Europe. That should not be allowed to happen. The idea of such a state is driven today by the forces of commercialisation and must be resisted.

Q. In a lot of countries populist-racist political parties are gaining ground as never before. Immigration is seen as the most important problem facing the Western nations, and borders, which were opened in recent decades, may be closed again. Also, more and more people are convinced that we should be less generous with the developing world, and first solve our own problems. How are we to handle these populist-racist political parties? Sincere politicians (they exist!) are totally desperate because they feel they lack the means to counteract the proposals of these populists for easy solutions to complicated problems. (July/August 2011)

A. It will take Maitreya Himself to provide 'the answer' to this most vexing problem. The fundamental issue can only be resolved through sharing.

Q. Is it possible to believe that humanity, in a short span of time, will create universal peace and stop producing arms? Can we hope to see this day, shortly? (March 2009)

A. There is certainly a very large decision to be made by humanity, and there are many reactionary forces in the world resistant to change. War and the production of armaments is a very lucrative business for some people who will resist change to the last. The present world economic collapse (presented as a 'downturn' or 'recession') signals the end of the old order, and is already bringing about a change in attitude among many people, young and old. When these same people hear Maitreya speak of the need to simplify and share resources to attain peace through justice, they will respond willingly to His call. His teaching and advocacy will inspire a huge response of desire for sharing, justice and thus peace. It is up to us. We have to want peace enough to relinquish the past and work for the one humanity. I am sure we shall do so.

Q. Are any governments beginning to think about sharing? (March 2007)

A. None of the governments of today are involved in the process of sharing the world's resources. It is the one thing that could save the world yet it is never taken as a serious idea. Every other method has been tried and has failed, and this has inevitably led to hardship and war.

Q. Set against the past destructive tendencies of the UK government, recent pronouncements in the UK seem to be in line with Maitreya's priorities, in terms of debt relief, the Commission on Africa, etc. Could your Master give an assessment of the state of consciousness of the nation? (Question from Benjamin Creme's lecture in London) (July/August 2006)

A. The British nation, according to my Master, is one of the more advanced.

Audience member: We all know it!

A. It may be known in a way that is not true, and not known in a way that is true. That is the point. The differences among the nations are minuscule. However, there are three old nations, which, because of their age, are somewhat more developed than others. They are Britain, France and Japan.

Audience member: What about Germany?

A. Germany is a very young nation. It is a very old people, but as a unified nation it is young.

Western powers are at least beginning to focus their attention on Africa, relieving some of the debt and some of the worst conditions of the day-to-day life of a lot of Africans. While nothing like enough, it is a sign that they are beginning to respond to the energies of Maitreya.

These energies have been pouring into the world for at least 25 years but it takes time to absorb and then act on them. At last, humanity has absorbed enough, the old patterns have disintegrated enough, to allow a new outlook and initiative that is being brought forward, mainly by Gordon Brown, the Chancellor of the Exchequer in the UK.

Q. Which country or countries are responding most positively to the new energies of Aquarius? (November 2006)
A. Britain, France, the Netherlands, Sweden, Norway, Finland, New Zealand, Brazil, Spain, Mexico.

Q. Are we facing the end of hypercapitalism? (November 2008)
A. Yes. According to the Masters the best ratio for successful, stable, fair government is: socialism 70 per cent, capitalism 30 per cent. At the present time the ratio in the US is 95 per cent capitalism, 5 per cent socialism. In the UK it is 85 per cent capitalism, 15 per cent socialism. France and Germany

are much the same. The ratio in Scandinavia is about 40 per cent capitalism, 60 per cent socialism. For this reason the Scandinavian countries, except for Iceland, are the most stable and fair.

Q. What can we do to get rid of capitalism? (July/August 2010)

A. We will not get rid of capitalism. We will give it a place in our society. It is not necessary to think in extremes, in black and white. No one ever thinks of these working together but Maitreya puts it this way: think of a cart. If you only have one wheel – whether capitalism or socialism – it will not go. All economic structures of the future will retain the balance of socialism and capitalism. Today there is no country in the world that has the balance right. From the Masters' point of view, the best balance is 30 per cent capitalism and 70 per cent socialism.

Which countries are most stable? The Scandinavian countries. Their balance is around 60 per cent capitalism to 40 per cent socialism.* That is still quite far off the best balance but it makes for a more stable society, which has no great wealth or poverty. It makes for a stable society with stable government.

One of the major problems from the economic point of view is that one of the most powerful countries, America, is 95 per cent capitalist to 5 per cent socialist. In Europe it is somewhat less: between 80 and 85 per cent capitalist to 15-20 per cent socialist. You can see how far off the major nations are and therefore how far out of balance the world is. Japan is about 80 per cent capitalist and 20 per cent socialist. It is not a question of either/or; it is the right balance of both.

[* This ratio is different from the previous answer that was given two years earlier (November 2008). The ratios change as the political situation of a nation changes. It is fluid.]

Q. The world's economic state seems more unstable and unsustainable than ever. Can you comment on the current crisis? (September 2011)

A. This economic crisis, worldwide, is inevitable. It is a symptom of the fact that the old economic principles, which have been in force for several centuries now, no longer work. The world has changed. The hearts and minds of men everywhere have changed – more or less. The countries making up the whole are at too disparate levels for the economic cohesion essential for stability. It is a sure sign, predicted by Maitreya long ago, that only sharing and justice can provide the right way into the future.

Q. There is a general economic crisis taking various forms across different parts of the world, and current leaders seem bereft of ideas. On the one hand they are printing money and on the other they are passing austerity measures. The financial organisations such as banks and corporations continue to be excessively powerful. What urgent steps should be taken now? (September 2011)

A. There is only one way to solve our political and economic problems – to bring peace and prosperity to all. Only the acceptance of the Oneness of humanity and the implementation of sharing and social justice will give us the trust that is necessary for peace. Whatever financial manipulations we try, nothing that does not implement sharing and justice will bring the peace which is necessary for survival.

Q. I read that Maitreya, your Master and you yourself think that commercialisation is destructive. Why? The world has always traded. (October 2011)

A. There is a difference between 'commerce', for example, trading, and the effect of commercialisation. Trading is a legitimate way of exchanging goods and, as you say, has been carried out for untold ages. Commercialisation is a situation in which making money (profit) enters every possible field of human activity. Even the provision of healthcare and education becomes subject to this gross materialism.

Today, commercialisation knows no bounds and cannot be contained. Every service is considered as a commodity, which can be bought and sold, at will. This degrading practice is at the heart of our problems today.

Q. How will countries that are struggling financially now be able to provide for their populations as the world's economic system collapses? Millions are already hungry and now more and more people in the affluent West are also beginning to feel the pinch. (November 2011)

A. The world has to see that this is inevitable. It is the 'wilderness experience'. Nothing will radically change unless people see this and look for an alternative way of living: that is, adopting sharing and thus justice and peace.

Q. The final demise of this economic system is painfully slow due, of course, to ongoing manipulation such as bailouts, debt ceiling increases and 'slash-and-burn' policies to public services and welfare systems etc. Will there come a time, very soon, when the markets finally bottom out and this slow death finally ends as the global markets and economy burn to the ground? (November 2011)

A. Yes. You might call this slow but actually, seen dispassionately, it is remarkably fast.

Q. Will it take a stock-market crash to really get the changes moving with regard to transforming the World Trade Organisation, the International Monetary Fund, the World Bank, the United Nations Security Council and so on? (March 2007)

A. I think it would take a serious disturbance in the existing stock markets, not necessarily a total crash, but a very serious disturbance of the norm to shift the opinion of the major governments – the G8 governments – to bring about these other reforms. Nothing will happen to the World Bank, the International Monetary Fund and so on until there is a major disturbance of the economic 'realities' of the present. It is reality we want. The whole thing is fantasy and we want the light of day. That will come when economic pressures are strong enough.

Q. Will the energies of Aquarius ever be great enough to rid the world of currency, monetary and economic systems and money interests that cause war and prevent the peace and sharing of which you speak? (October 2010)

A. Yes, it must be very soon indeed before we destroy the world. It is urgent. We have to create peace. A small war could become a big war. It would be nuclear and destroy all life forms. We therefore have no alternative to sharing.

Q. One year ago [January 2010], Maitreya stepped forward to begin His mission. Since then, He has appeared on US television 28 times. The US is worse off now than it was a year ago. So is the rest of the world. Is Maitreya's mission failing? Why aren't things getting better? Why isn't there a more noticeable galvanisation of the masses to His presence and message? Thank you for your response and your good work. (March 2011)

A. It is true that, economically, everything is, or is getting, worse. This is the inevitable result of trying to continue in the old ways that no longer work. Maitreya does not come to make the old methods more tolerable but to show the way (the only way) into the future. Humanity has the means in its hands if it wants to survive: Sharing, Justice and Freedom for all is the only answer to our troubles. As to a response to

His ideas, look what has happened in Egypt (the 'Arab Spring').

Q. Is Maitreya going to inspire us to action, such as with sharing, based on an experience He will give us of our oneness? Otherwise, will humanity be motivated to share? (January/February 1996)

The answer to that is, yes and no. Maitreya is not going to force anyone to share, but He is going to talk about the necessity of sharing as the only way to produce a rational economic system that will create justice. It is the injustice of the present system that is bringing it to its knees. It is ending because the age that brought it into being has ended. It is a decaying, corrupt, crystallised form that does good to a few and to the many a great deal of harm. Of course it also does harm to the few to whom it seems to be doing good. It is poisoning, dividing, and threatening the world, so it has to go. All of this will be spelled out by Maitreya. If that does not inspire us with the idea of sharing, then nothing will.

Maitreya will also release His energy – the Christ Principle – in tremendous potency. As Maitreya Himself has said: "It will be as if I embrace the world. People will feel it even physically." If that energy flowing through us, plus the words of Maitreya analysing the economic situation and the harm it is doing to planetary life, do not motivate us to share, then nothing else will. If it does not motivate humanity, then we will not learn to share and we will destroy the world. We have it in our own hands.

This questioner obviously does not have too much faith in the rest of humanity. "Otherwise, will humanity be motivated to share?" Humanity will be motivated to share by the analysis given by Maitreya of what will happen if we do not, and also by the experience of the Christ Principle. That is the experience which He will give us. The Christ Principle embodies the sense of oneness. It is the magnetic energy of love whose nature is oneness. Love is, above all, the inclusive energy. It is that which unites, draws together, the building blocks of creation and holds them magnetically in oneness.

Q. How will it work in practice? Will the changes occur on a national basis? For instance, in the US, will we say: "We need to change our priorities."? Or will it happen internationally through the UN or some other forum? (July/August 1993)

A. I would suggest it is a combination of both. The UN will become the major debating chamber of the world. All world problems will be debated there and resolutions passed that will implement the new system. An entirely new UN agency will be set up specifically to oversee the process of sharing the world's resources. But I must emphasise that we have free will. Nothing will be forced on humanity. When humanity of its own free will accepts the principle of sharing and asks Maitreya and His group of Masters, how do we set about sharing, then we will find that the plan is already there. There is a group of high initiates who have worked out with the Masters over many years a series of interrelated plans that will solve the redistribution problems which today are at the heart of the world's economic problems. It is really a problem of redistribution of resources.

That redistribution will result from a change of consciousness. Humanity is approaching a point where it is undergoing a great shift in consciousness, beginning to recognise itself in relation to each other and to cosmos, to nature, to what we generally call God, in an entirely new way. Maitreya says that everything, every single thing in cosmos, is interconnected. There is no break at any point. What we do to ourselves, we do to nature. What we do to nature, we are doing to ourselves as God, because we are reflections, points of consciousness of that total consciousness that we call God.

Throughout the whole of cosmos this process is enacted and re-enacted. Every thought, every action is setting into motion a cause. The effects stemming from these causes

95

make our lives. If we have an underground nuclear explosion, for example, we will certainly have an earthquake. Every effect stems from a cause.

Maitreya will emphasise – and we ought to know it by now, we have had thousands of years to understand it – that everything in life obeys the Law of Cause and Effect. We cannot go on creating wrong conditions and expect there will be no effects. If we create conditions of imbalance in a nation, inevitably we get crime. Just making a stronger police force or army will not solve the problem. We have to combat the source of the crime – inequality, imbalance. The whole process of evolution is moving towards oneness, fusion, synthesis. Market forces, which are based on division, separation and competition, act against the evolutionary process. That is why Maitreya calls them "the forces of evil". They have their place, but only a very limited place. When they are followed blindly, they lead inevitably to destruction.

Q. Will Maitreya be openly advising humanity? (July/August 1993)

A. Yes. He will come forward as the World Teacher for all groups, religious and non-religious alike. He will be looked to by religious groups as their expected Teacher – the Christ for Christians, Maitreya Buddha for Buddhists, the Messiah of the Jews, the Imam Mahdi for the Muslims, and Krishna for the Hindus. In fact He is really a teacher, an educator, for the whole of humanity, showing us how to become what we are, spiritual beings, and therefore how to create the environment in which that spirituality can be expressed. It cannot be expressed in the midst of these divisions and separations, this competition based on market forces.

THE PEOPLE'S VOICE

THE PATH TO UNITY

by the Master —, through Benjamin Creme

When the history of this unique time is written, men will realise, perhaps for the first time, how important, how central, have been the recent events in the Middle East. In an astonishing six months, following the example of the people of Tunisia and Egypt, the inhabitants of many Middle Eastern countries, subdued, and locked into centuries-old tribal dictatorial regimes, have risen and demanded their right to freedom and democracy, to social justice and work. What media call 'the Arab Spring' is costing many lives and much suffering for these courageous people who die willingly for freedom for their brothers and children. They are called, and are indeed, martyrs.

From now on, this same phenomenon will manifest throughout the world. Already, many peoples are organising themselves to do likewise. A blueprint for change has caught the imagination of many millions and soon will command the attention of the world. Men have understood that, when organised and brave, they are invincible. Nothing can halt this movement for change. It embodies the concepts of the future and of the Plan. Maitreya has given it voice, which is now the voice of the peoples of the world.

The old order seeks in every way to halt the progress of this movement for change, but it cannot stand for ever against the principles of life: ever changing, ever remaking its form to better express the nature of that life. Thus is it today, and thus the old will wither and the new shoots flourish, as men seek to express and manifest better the principles of the New Time: sharing, justice, right relationship, love and unity.

Man, verily, is on his way. Naught can halt his further progress if he thinks in terms of Unity. All men seek Unity but are confused by different paths. Hold ever before you the principles of Unity and Love, and the way discloses itself.

Thus spoke Maitreya in Cairo, in Tahrir Square. The best of those who heard Him will lead their brothers and sisters and show them the way, the simple way to Brotherhood and Peace, Justice and manifested Love.

(*Share International*, July/August 2011)

YOUTH AT THE HELM

by the Master —, through Benjamin Creme

This year, 2012, is one of great importance. It is essential that the impetus of the Arab Dawn, and its repercussions worldwide, be not lost. The Voice of the People, so vigorous and confident now, must continue to ring out through all the world, affirming Sharing and Justice as the only way to engender trust and a safer world for all. The remedy for men's ills is so simple, so easy of achievement, yet so difficult for many to grasp. Men must realise that every other method has been tried and has failed, ending inevitably in war.

Today, let all be assured, another major war would be nuclear, and would destroy, utterly, all life on Earth. Today, also, there are forces who are already planning how best to survive such annihilation, all to no avail. What can, and should, humanity do?

Broadly speaking, the governments today are organisations of elderly men who know no other way to work and govern than the ways of their youth, the ways of the past. They have little sense of why their methods no longer work. They know nothing of the new energies and impulses which flood the world today, and are baffled and betrayed by their inability to control events.

To a large extent, today, the People's Voice is the voice of the young. Governments, and the media under their control, largely ignore or vilify the voices and aspirations of the young; yet it is the young who have the answers, who understand that humanity is One, who call for fairness, for justice and sharing, and an end to war. The voice of such young people can never be silenced, and will not for long be ignored. The Voice of the People, young and old, will drown the whimpers of the men of money and lead humanity to the New Dawn. So will it be.

(*Share International*, April 2012)

AWAKENING OF THE PEOPLE

Q. How can people obtain more diversity in political representation? (March 2007)

A. The people have to make their demands known and act. You have to act. Maitreya says: "Nothing happens by itself. Man must act and implement his will." If we want the process of sharing, we have to force the governments to accept it. The governments are there to serve the people and they will go on serving the people in the way that they do. But if you want change, if you want more representation, you have to force it on the governments. I am sure people do want more representation, which means taking some of the power out of the few hands which in most cases run the governments in the world. They are not going to give up their power voluntarily. But when the people demand it, when every day there is a march, thousands, hundreds of thousands of people who fill the squares and the streets of the towns and refuse to move, then they can force the hand of any government. We have seen it already.

Q. Does a constitution guarantee people's rights? (March 2007)

A. It depends on the system. In Britain we do not have a constitution, but we have a relatively fair system of government.

In America people talk much about the constitution and the rights of the people but in practice the rights of the people enshrined in the constitution are infringed by the present administration. Every autocracy in the world behaves in the same way whatever the constitution says.

Q. Were the Buddhist monks who were protesting against the government in Burma inspired by Maitreya? (March 2008)

A. No, they are not inspired by Maitreya, not directly, but they are inspired by the energy that Maitreya pours into the world. This creates the desire in people everywhere for freedom, for justice, for, in other words, right relationship. If there is no freedom or justice there cannot be peace or right relationship.

You can see this all over the world. People everywhere are demanding their rights: freedom, justice and the sharing of the world's resources. All of this comes from their response to the energy and, to some extent, to the thoughts and ideas of Maitreya from a subtle level.

You will see, when Maitreya speaks on television and radio, how many thousands or millions of people will say: "That is what we want. We want to do this; we want right relationship. We want the end of war and terrorism and hunger," and so on.

Humanity, then, is stimulated and activated to demand these things. In this way the educated, focused will of humanity creates a world public opinion against war, against terrorism, and calls for justice and sharing. Thus Maitreya does not impose, but humanity, stimulated by Maitreya, does the work.

Millions are marching already throughout the world, not every day nor week, but this action will grow more and more until the governments of the world will be faced with thousands and sometimes millions of people demanding their rights, demanding work or peace or sharing and justice, until the governments have to concede.

Maitreya is stimulating this all the time. He goes to every big march. At every big demonstration Maitreya is there for part of the time.

Q. To some critics, marches, protests and demonstrations are anarchic acts undermining the true mechanisms of democracy. Your insights, please. (July/August 2008)

A. It is true that rising prices of food and oil and local shortages of staple foods are the main cause as yet, rather

101

than more abstract international causes like Justice and Peace, but it is a step in the direction required.

Q. Twenty years ago there was a huge surge of people power and the overturning of the political order, the end of the Cold War – a definite change in the world's political climate. Suddenly freedom and new possibilities filled the air. (1) What caused these amazing changes? (2) Do you think it has led to a better world? (3) When communism collapsed it left a vacuum for commercialisation and its attendant problems, such as widespread criminality. Has life improved in the former Soviet Union? (December 2009)

A. (1) The ending of the Cold War was foretold by Maitreya and was set in motion by Him when He suggested to Mr Gorbachev to go to America and talk peace with President Reagan. It also included Maitreya's advice to Mr Gorbachev to open up the Soviet Union to *perestroika* (structural reform) and *glasnost* (liberation). Maitreya's advice was carried out by Mr Gorbachev but unfortunately in the process he lost his position. (2) Yes. (3) Overall, yes.

Q. In recent years, Central and South America have seen the rise of people's movements that have challenged and effectively changed the status quo. These movements have elected into power Hugo Chavez in Venezuela, Evo Morales in Bolivia and Rafael Correa in Ecuador, among others. Are these some of the positive changes that have come about due to the new energies, including those released by Maitreya, into the world? (March 2007)

A. Yes. They are also the expression of the awakening of humanity, at the grassroots level, to the need for the transformation of the world's economy.

Q. Does the US administration fear people power – both within the USA and in Latin America? (January/February 2006)

A. Yes, but the US administration is not alone in fearing the power of the people. More and more, all governments are becoming aware of this added threat to their dominion. They will try to curb it in every way they dare, but they cannot stop the greatest power on earth from rising and fulfilling its destiny.

Q. What is the relation between the recent events in the Middle East and the appearance and support of Maitreya and the Hierarchy of Masters? (April 2011)

A. The people of the Middle East, and of the world in general, are beginning to find their voice. This is not only in response to the ideas of Maitreya but was predicted by Him.

Q. Maitreya says that "power will come from the people". (1) Is this "people's power" that we are now witnessing in Egypt, the kind of power that Maitreya talks about? (2) Will this kind of movement now begin to spread across the globe with more strength, as we move (as your Master says) nearer the Day of Declaration? (April 2011)

A. (1) Yes. (2) Yes.

Q. The ongoing news of the Arab Spring is wonderful but how sad if the countries revert back to old ways of inequality for women. Already talks of Sharia Law are in the news and sadly women seem to be low on the priority list. Is this something that only Maitreya can deal with? (December 2011)

A. It would be sad indeed if Arab groups attained the present promise of freedom and democracy without extending it to all Arab women. Personally I do not expect this to be the case in, for example, Egypt or Tunisia or Libya.

Many 'liberated' Arab women do not oppose much of Sharia Law, seeing it as rational and useful in many cases and they're even prepared to limit their own freedoms if necessary. One has to remember that freedom for women in many Arab countries has been for long non-existent and that change takes time.

If we believe in democracy we have to also believe that Muslims have the right to make their own choice of laws. I have no doubt that some of the most severe aspects of Sharia Law, particularly as used in places like Afghanistan, will take Maitreya's breadth of view to moderate.

Q. A recent demonstration and protest by Coptic Christians in Cairo, Egypt, was brutally suppressed by the army in power. Steps towards democracy seem to be slow and resisted by the government. Will true democracy really come to pass in Egypt? (November 2011)

A. Yes indeed, but it will take more time. The forces against democracy – the army in power and the right-wing financial interests – are still very powerful. The overthrowing of Hosni Mubarak was itself a miracle that has reverberated throughout the Middle East and is inspiring the people's voice throughout the world, including the US.

Q. The people of Egypt and of Japan have shown the world (through the recent extraordinary events) lessons of discipline, equanimity and collective support. What factors make them so exemplary? Is it their history, for example? (May 2011)

A. Yes, mainly. Also, in Egypt, Maitreya spent three weeks in Cairo, much of the time with the protestors in Tahrir Square. In Japan, Maitreya and other Masters spent much time during the catastrophe (earthquakes, tsunamis and nuclear power plants disaster) saving and consoling the people.

Q. I have read some of your criticisms of the developed world in regard to world hunger. Besides writing to my Congressman, which from experience does practically no good, what else can I, just one man, do? (January/February 2006)

A. Keep writing and marching and demonstrating that you are a man of feeling and heart. You are one man but there are millions like you in the world.

Q. (1) Do you think we will ever see people power in the USA equal to that now playing out in the Middle East and North Africa? (2) If so, what do Americans have to protest about? (May 2011)

A. (1) Yes, most certainly. The world awaits the manifestation of the American soul, which, I believe, will happen after the Day of Declaration. However, it was people power that forced the USA to withdraw its troops from Vietnam and it was people power which ended 'apartheid' in the USA. (2) The USA is enormous and has a population of about 300 million with diverse political and economic points of view, giving plenty of reasons for some groups to protest for or against.

Q. Do you think the new populist movement in the USA, which started as 'Occupy Wall Street' and has now spread rapidly to other cities, is a viable movement? (November 2011)

A. Yes. It is the beginning of the USA's transformation.

Q. Is the 'Occupy' movement – which is springing up around the US now in response to the Occupy Wall Street demonstration – the kind of expression of people power that Maitreya is looking to galvanise and spread around the world? (November 2011)

A. It is part of it. At least in the beginning different groups in different countries will use different methods of bringing it about.

Q. The Occupy movement in the United States has been criticised by some people for not having a specific set of demands that would pressure the US government to make specific changes. Others say that the Occupy movement is not a political movement, and that they are trying to create something new, and more broadly based to change society fundamentally. What is your view of this? (December 2011)

A. I agree with this second idea. There would be no end to the demands and therefore no action if that was the only intention.

Q. To my mind the Occupy movement (which I support 100 per cent as one of the '99 per cent') in London has created a distraction by being camped outside St Paul's Cathedral. Surely the issue is social and economic injustice, corruption, profit being put before people, and not the location of the protestor's camp? However, being outside St Paul's Cathedral, London, is making the clergy think about their stance vis à vis money and ethical trading and investment. Jesus drove the money lenders and traders out of the temple. What is your opinion about the situation? (December 2011)

A. This location for the Occupy movement camp may not be altogether appropriate but it has resulted in an unusual demonstration of unity with the occupiers by the Church authorities, and anything that brings the Church closer to supporting the people is to be welcomed.

Q. What lies behind the explosion of violence in many places around the UK in early August 2011? (September 2011)

A. Social injustice. The ever-widening gap between the richest and the poorest. Bad housing, unemployment, vicious cuts in welfare and public services.

The trigger to all of this social upheaval, which remains ready to erupt at any time, was the shooting, by the police, of a young man who was apparently armed. The police later admitted that his gun had not been fired, having first stated that he had shot at them. People have lost trust in the police, have lost trust in Parliament, and feel they have nothing to lose. They took the wrong step, to my mind, of burning and trashing their own communities and others.

Q. Is it just a case of opportunistic criminality? (September 2011)

A. There was an element of that, in the general excitement of destruction.

Q. What are the solutions to such situations? (September 2011)

A. As ever, sharing and justice.

Q. It is clear that Maitreya and the Masters encourage people power – I see reading **Share International**. *But do They condone mindless violence and destruction such as seen recently in England?* (October 2011)

A. "Mindless violence and destruction" is not a demonstration of people power but of destructive power. Hierarchy would never encourage or condone violence or destruction.

Q. You talk about people power, and there have been a lot of peace marches. Are they actually having an impact? It seems that people don't attend them, so do they actually make a difference? (May 2007)

A. There was a march quite recently in London, and the organisers said that about 100,000 people attended. The police eventually admitted about 10,000 had taken part. My Master said the organisers were not far from the truth, it was between 90,000 and 100,000. The police always lie about the numbers taking part in a march. It is just simple manipulation by the police for governmental reasons, to make out that the people are under control. It is to put people off marching because they will say: "What's the use?" However, you can only see part of the march at any given time, the bit you are in. You have no idea of its extent. It is usually that the organisers put the best figure on it and maybe exaggerate, but this time they don't seem to have exaggerated at all. It is important to maintain a growing number of marches, not now and again but continually, and these sustained demonstrations will have a gradual impact on government thinking.

It is difficult for us to estimate the value of such demonstrations but the Masters are in no doubt that they are very powerful levers of change. We must organise them more and more frequently and with even greater numbers. 'People power' will transform the world.

Q. I am 23 and from Egypt. I've followed you for several years now and I can't wait for the change to come! I see the changes in the form of revolutions. (1) But I ask myself, when does the change come in the form of a miracle? Every spiritual site I go to, everybody who channels, is saying it is near, a lot is changing. My question is, when do believers (or someone like me), notice that it's at the beginning? Every normal person should notice that this is not normal. (2) As I am a Muslim, I am interested if Mohammed (pbuh) is also, like the Master Jesus, on Earth right now as a Master who is going to help us? (November 2011)

A. (1) You look for signs that things are happening now. Do you not see what is happening throughout the Middle East and further afield? Do you not remember, in Egypt, Cairo, Tahrir Square, only a few months ago something that is beginning to happen more and more worldwide? Maitreya Himself spent many hours in that square over three weeks inspiring and safe-guarding the people of all religions, teaching them to protect and look after each other as an inspiration to the world. It is the people everywhere, raising their voices, who will change, and are changing the world, even now. (2) The Master who was Mohammed is not in incarnation, but working through His disciple to reform Islam. Mohammed received His inspiration and teaching from Jesus. They are brothers.

Q. Certain countries are determined to stop immigration and to that end they build walls to keep would-be illegal immigrants from entering, or they round up and deport people already settled. It is just over 20 years ago that the Berlin Wall came down thanks to people power. What can be done to prevent governments from building separation walls and/or deporting people in large numbers? (October 2010)

A. By the same method: people power!

Q. If people have ideals but do not act on them what can be done to rid us of complacency, which humanity seems to suffer from? (October 2010)

A. Indeed. Complacency is the disease. Money is an energy – it is neither good nor bad. It can be used for good or harm. People think that money is the root of all evil, but complacency, which stems from a sense of separation, is the *real* sin.

People know what's going on in the world. They know people are starving to death. People in big rich nations like America and in Europe know people are dying. We used to see them dying on our television screens but that is no longer shown because we would turn off and so miss the commercials. Nevertheless, people are dying from starvation all the time. Five million children die each year from diseases related to malnutrition. This should not be happening. We have the answer to all these illnesses. There is a surplus of food in the world of 12 per cent per capita. It is simply not distributed. The answer to the economic problem is the redistribution of the resources of the world. This would create universal justice and, therefore, peace. It is the only way to peace.

Q. (1) Do you think people power will succeed in Libya and Syria? (2) What would be the most practical solution in each country? (June 2011)

A. (1) Yes, eventually. (2) The problems and state of readiness in each country are different. Eventually, throughout the world, people power, inspired by Maitreya and under the banner of freedom, sharing and justice, will succeed.

Q. Should dictators and despots be brought to justice? (June 2011)

A. Personally, I do not think so. It solves nothing and simply prolongs the lust for revenge.

Q. Perhaps in a spirit of forgiveness old autocratic figures ought to be given asylum and amnesty? (June 2011)

A. Yes, I agree.

Q. (1) Should Colonel Gaddafi and his sons be charged with 'crimes against humanity' or given asylum somewhere? (2) If asylum, what message does that send to other dictators? (October 2011)

A. (1) I would vote for asylum. If Gaddafi and his sons were charged in a world court they (or their followers) would become martyrs. It is better that the memory of their misdeeds and policies of terror are not allowed to be glorified but are quickly superseded, forgotten and forgiven. It should not be forgotten that there are still neo-Nazi groups in Germany and elsewhere.

(2) I do not think that asylum would give encouragement to existing dictators. The removal from power is for them sufficient loss. The thought of asylum could even encourage them to go.

Q. Should people power try to bring down the economic structure of its own country? (November 2011)

A. People power is not about 'bringing down' the economic structure of any particular country. It is about the winning of freedom, justice and peace for the people of that country. The ultimate aim should always be kept in mind, which is the establishment of freedom, justice and peace throughout the world. It should be obvious that a radical reorganisation of the world's economic structures must take place for this to be achieved. Sharing, you will find, is the paramount mechanism for this achievement.

Q. Do even the most dedicated activists working to change the current economic, political and social systems, and those working to save the environment, really have any practical, feasible answers? (November 2011)

A. Yes, very much so. Sharing and justice that will transform life for everybody and guarantee the end of war is the aim of everybody, whether stated or not.

Q. Currently what is the most important work that the World Teacher is carrying out? (December 2011)

A. From our point of view, the awakening of the spiritual nature of humanity to manifest and so to change the world for the better.

SAVING PLANET EARTH

SAVING THE PLANET

by the Master —, through Benjamin Creme

When mankind realises how serious is the ecological imbalance of their planetary home, they must take the steps so urgently needed to remedy the situation. If men were to fail to respond with sufficient resolution they would be guilty of surrendering the planet to slow but inevitable destruction. What, then, the legacy to hand on to their children? That this self-destruction should not prevail all must act together, and make the necessary sacrifices. This will entail a complete change in attitude to the integrity of the planet and what are seen as the needs of men today.

It will not be easy for some to countenance the changes needed but only by such change can the life of the planet be assured. Already, deep inroads have been made into the essential stock of trees on Earth. Deforestation has caused a growing loss of oxygen and the rise of carbon gases. This is now at a critical stage and requires immediate action.

The reality of global warming is now dawning on the minds of millions, yet, despite the overwhelming evidence some still deny the actions of men are the cause.

We, your Elder Brothers, can say with full conviction that the actions of men are responsible for eighty per cent of global warming.

Maitreya, you will find, will not be long in bringing this urgent problem to man's attention. He will face men with the alternatives: the beneficial results of action now, on the one hand, and the destruction which would ensue from doing nothing, or too little, on the other. Thus, the decision is man's alone.

When men understand this they will indeed rally to the cause. They will see that the future for their children

113

depends on action now, and will elicit from Maitreya and His group the necessary steps to take. Maitreya will advocate a simpler form of living, one more in keeping with the reality of the planet's situation. When enough people are convinced that this is necessary there will be a growing movement to simplify throughout the planet. This will proceed with quite unusual speed, so inspired by the need for change will millions be. Thus will the gravest dangers facing Planet Earth be somewhat countered. This will encourage many and boost their readiness for further changes.

Faced with the dilemma of necessary change men will come to realise the inevitability of accepting the principle of sharing. Only sharing will make these changes practical and possible. Only through sharing can the bounty of Planet Earth be successfully used. Only through sharing can this bounty be correctly husbanded. Only thus can the Planet itself live in harmony with its environment and with its inhabitants.

(Share International, May 2007)

MAN'S RESPONSIBILITY

by the Master —, through Benjamin Creme

From the earliest times, mankind has feared the natural disturbances of our planetary home. Cataclysms of unimaginable ferocity have destroyed huge areas of the Earth's surface over and over again. This fact is hard for many to accept and raises, always, grave doubts in the minds of many religious people about the veracity of God's love for humanity. How can we believe in a loving God who allows thousands of people to be killed in earthquakes, tsunamis and the rest? Were humanity to understand their own involvement in such planetary destruction, they could play a significant role in preventing its occurrence.

The Earth's crust, as it has evolved over the ages, is not single and evenly spread around the world. As is well known, it takes the form of various plates at different depths, which overlap and are in relatively constant movement. Countries and cities which lie on or near the plate edge, or fault-lines, are consequently subjected to earthquakes and, if near oceanic regions, tsunamis. It is not a question of God's love failing humanity but of seismic pressure which must be released. What, we may ask, causes seismic pressure to grow to such a destructive extent?

Elemental Devas (or Angelic forces) oversee the mechanism by which these colossal energies act or are modified. The Earth is a living Entity and responds to the impact of these forces in various ways. One major source of impact comes directly from humanity. As humanity, in its usual competitive way, creates tension through wars, and political and economic crisis – that is when we are out of equilibrium – so too do the Devic lives go out of equilibrium. The inevitable result is earthquakes, volcanic eruptions and tsunamis. We are responsible.

How then to end this cycle of destruction? Humanity has the means but so far lacks the will to change. We must see ourselves as One, each man and woman a reflection of the Divine, brothers and sisters, sons and daughters of the One Father. We must banish war for ever from this Earth; we must share the resources of this planet which belong to all. We must learn to live in harmony with the planet itself to know a future of harmony with each other.

Maitreya has come to show men the way, and to galvanise man's actions. Across the globe, men are finding their voice and calling for justice and freedom. Many have died to claim their right, God given, to freedom and justice. His call is for all men and women everywhere to see themselves as He sees them, as Divine, Sons and Daughters of Divinity Itself.

(*Share International*, April 2011)

GLOBAL WARMING, NATURAL DISASTERS AND KARMA

Q. "Today 56 newspapers in 45 countries take the unprecedented step of speaking with one voice through a common editorial. We do so because humanity faces a profound emergency." This was the unprecedented step taken by editors of newspapers around the world on the eve of the Copenhagen Climate Summit in December 2009. Was this combined effort inspired by the Spiritual Hierarchy? If so, which Master was it? Should we look forward to more such historical occurrences in the coming months?
(January/February 2010)

A. Yes, Maitreya. This kind of action by groups of people in varied branches of society will increase and take form in the coming months and years. The media is the mouthpiece of the people reflecting the people's longing for action to save the planet. This kind of action will continue in one way or another until that initiative is no longer needed.

Q. Following the failure of leaders to arrive at a far-reaching agreement at the December 2009 UN climate conference in Copenhagen, allegations have surfaced concerning the reasons for the failure.

Was it due to (1) China, and to some extent India, with economies that are still growing, protecting their own economic interests; (2) industrial and corporate interests, represented primarily by the US Chamber of Commerce, preventing any measures that would interfere with their freedom to pollute at will; (3) the Danish Prime Minister, desperate for a result of some sort, brokering a weak and partial agreement among a few selected countries?
(January/February 2010)

A. (1) Yes. (2) Yes. (3) No.

Q. (1) Do you personally think that the recent explosion on the oil rig in the Gulf of Mexico and the resulting environmental catastrophe is the final coffin nail, so-to-speak, in the call for more off-shore drilling in America? (2) May I ask how many hundreds of thousands, or millions, of gallons of oil have flowed into the ocean from the broken oil pipe off the southern coast of the US at the time of your answering this question? (July/August 2010)

A. (1) No, I am sorry to say. I do not think so, given the constant lust for more oil of the American oil companies (for whom it is liquid gold) and a large section of the American public who have been conditioned to fear its demise. (2) Several millions. This accident is being heralded as the 'greatest catastrophe ever to have occurred in the USA'. I personally do not take this view. Several similar have occurred even within quite recent years in the USA, Europe and elsewhere. Nature has a wonderful way of absorbing and overcoming these accidents and usually within a few years, the life of the area affected goes back to normal.

Q. Was the explosion that sank the oil drilling rig in April 2010, which has resulted in colossal environmental damage off the eastern US coast, the result of karma and, if so, may I ask why? (July/August 2010)

A. No, it was an accident. Actually, it has not resulted in "colossal environmental damage" but in 'potential' environmental damage. Seen from Europe, President Obama (and he would normally have my vote) is overplaying his attempt to hold BP to account for every dollar of loss occurred. BP has already accepted responsibility and readiness to meet bonafide reasonable claims. I wonder if the American public knows that BP is half-owned by US investors.

Q. I know you have said that certain species of more 'primitive' animals are destined to die out. Is it also part of the Plan that so many species of birds, animals and aquatic animals will die out? Experts are warning that many are under threat of extinction because of the destructive effect of human activity on the environment. (May 2006)

A. It is true that environmental change caused by human activity is having a very destructive effect on many species of animals, birds and fish. However, the planned slow extinction of certain very ancient and primitive animals and fish has an evolutionary purpose and takes place under law. It is the result of the focused destructive aspect of the 1st ray.

Q. As the world media is aware, there have recently been thousands of bird and fish deaths. Conventional explanations have been offered that few people would accept. One of the less conventional explanations is that the magnetic poles may be shifting rapidly and allowing invasion of our lower atmosphere by hydrogen cyanide clouds that would instantaneously kill birds. This doesn't explain the fish deaths though. Another explanation is atmospheric experiments by Project HAARP. It is obvious that something that may affect all life may be in process.

My question to **Share International** *is this: from the viewpoint of the Spiritual Hierarchy, what is the primary cause or causes of this phenomenon?* (April 2011)

A. According to the information from the Spiritual Hierarchy, the magnetic poles are not shifting. The Masters say the causes are climatic and result from the vast quantities of torrential rain in various parts of the world. These rains not only cause floods but bring down many very toxic pollutants, including nuclear radiation, released into the atmosphere by every nuclear power station.

Q. Can you explain why, if global warming is a major problem, Maitreya has "brought the Earth a little closer to the Sun"? Doesn't that exacerbate the warming, and if so, can we assume that whatever climate changes do occur will not in the end prove more deleterious than if Maitreya had not performed this rather bizarre-seeming action? (June 2006)

A. Twenty per cent of global warming is caused by the Earth having been brought a little nearer to the sun. Eighty per cent is caused by our misuse of resources and gas emissions. Why would Maitreya do this? One has to assume that it is under Law and for the benefit of humanity. It will render large areas of northern Europe, Asia, Canada and Russia, now largely icebound for most months of the year, extraordinarily fertile for growing food. It also reinforces the need for action on our part to limit global warming.

Q. Brazil is preparing to build a huge hydro-electric dam in the Amazon basin. Its construction will cost indigenous people their homes and their environment. A large area of the forest will be irreparably destroyed. Our planet is dependent on rainforests. Would this be a case where the Masters could intervene to save the forests? (October 2010)

A. No, that would be an infringement of humanity's free will and would never happen. It is really a case for a decision by the United Nations. Brazil is enormous and there are surely less destructive areas for such a dam.

Q. Indian activists have just succeeded in preventing the building of a large dam on the River Ganges. Were the activists right to fight against a scheme that would, after all, bring them many benefits? (October 2010)

A. Yes. It is a question of weighing the benefits against the destruction.

Q. Floods, droughts, fires, mudslides, volcanoes – the upheaval and destruction in the world today seem to have reached a new high level. Is this true? And is it all due to the karma of the particular countries involved? (October 2010)

A. Humanity is going through a period of great stress and disequilibrium. The Devas who control the forces of the environment are forced out of equilibrium, hence the upheaval and destruction. Some of this destruction does indeed result from the karma of particular countries.

Q. Was the cyclone that hit Burma natural, and were the earthquakes in China natural or man-made? (July/August 2008)

A. No, they were not natural and they were not directly man-made or manipulated. Nor were they the karmic result of the government of Burma or China's misdeeds. They are the result of tension and the resulting stress that unleashes forces which cannot be contained.

For example, humanity does not understand the Law of Cause and Effect, the Law of Harmlessness. We have tremendous tension in the world today because of the Iraq invasion – a totally illegal, unnecessary and ghastly war, costly in human lives. That war, the invasion by the Americans and the British, has created extraordinary tension in the world. That, as well as the war in Afghanistan and American pressure on Iran, causes inevitable fear across the world. So people are living in a state of tension partly because of the great cosmic energies but also because of the actions of powerful individuals. And people watch in silence. This country [Japan] watches in silence because you are allies of America. But all nations of the world must raise their voices against this trampling on other countries by America.

America is a great nation and will become a greater nation but it is sadly out of step with its destiny. It is playing with forces it does not understand. It is a young, powerful and extremely arrogant nation. It is the arrogance of youth, especially strong youth. It is time that the older, wiser nations of the world raised their voices against the actions of America.

The best way to do that is to encourage the acceptance of sharing. Sharing and justice will bring tranquillity and balance to the world.

When we are out of equilibrium – as we are now – the sub-human elemental forces, which organise the cyclones, earthquakes and so on, the forces of the planet itself, go out of equilibrium. Where you have regular tornadoes, they become massive; where you have regular earthquakes, they become massive earthquakes. The elemental forces respond to our stress. Humanity has to understand the connection that exists between all forces and all aspects of the planet.

Q. A 7.7 magnitude earthquake struck off the coast of Indonesia on 21 January 2006. Was this a natural event? (March 2006)

A. Yes.

Q. The state of Tennessee in the USA was hit by several tornadoes and extensive storm damage in the first two weeks of April 2006. Some areas were declared disasters by the federal government, and around 60 people lost their lives. (1) Was it karmic and was it in relation to a certain action?

Two events occurred at the time: in Gallatin, near Nashville, a man, his mother (or stepmother), his son and his dog were driving in their vehicle when a tornado directly hit them. The car was lifted almost five feet in the air and spun numerous times before landing almost 35 yards from where it was picked up. The velocity was such that the car crashed into a tree, which split, toppled and covered the car. Everyone in the car survived and the only injury was to the man, who suffered a cut to his ear. (2) Was this a miracle, and who was responsible for it? (3) In another incident, a man and his mother were hiding in a closet in their home when it was directly hit by a tornado. They held on to each other but were separated when the tornado destroyed the house and lifted them into the air. The man survived but his mother did not. Was this a miracle? (June 2006)

A. (1) Yes. The result of destructive actions in Iraq. (2) Yes. The Master Jesus. (3) Yes, by the Master Jesus.

Q. The earthquake that struck Haiti seems particularly cruel, as it is one of the poorest countries in the Western hemisphere. (1) Was the earthquake karmically caused, the natural movement of the Earth's tectonic plates, or some other reason? (2) Did the Masters prevent an even worse disaster from occurring there? (3) Were the Masters involved in helping the sick and dying in Haiti? (March 2010)

A. (1) It is karmic, the result of long tension between the poor of Haiti, the poorest people in all the Americas, and the long succession of despotic and corrupt leaders for decades in Haiti. (2) Yes. (3) As always, yes.

Q. The 9.0 magnitude earthquake that hit the north-eastern part of Japan on Friday, 11 March 2011, caused great loss of life and huge destruction. Nevertheless, was there Maitreya's divine intervention? (April 2011)

A. Yes, without which the suffering would have been far greater.

Q. It was reported that there was only 20-30 minutes between the earthquake and the time the tsunami reached shore. The Japanese were prepared for tsunamis of smaller scale, but never before experienced a tsunami of such magnitude, and a lot of people got caught. The death toll is still climbing. (1) Did those people who were swept away by the tsunami receive any divine intervention? (2) Did they suffer? (April 2011)

A. (1) Yes, many more were saved. (2) Strangely, no. Maitreya has the power to remove fear and pain.

Q. Did the Space Brothers in UFOs come to monitor and help with the nuclear power plants accident in Fukushima? (April 2011)

A. They came to monitor and help if necessary.

Q. Two days after the earthquake and tsunami hit Japan, various video clips could be seen on online video sites, YouTube, for example, purporting to show UFO activity immediately after the earthquake struck. Are the Space People working over the nuclear power stations to help curb radiation leaks? (April 2011)

A. Yes. These nuclear power stations were, and are, a major concern.

*Q. Having read answers in **Share International** over the years about the ways in which Maitreya and the Masters help people during disasters I hope you can assure readers that the same is true once again in Japan and also Libya?* (April 2011)

A. Yes indeed, within Karmic Law, the Masters are always first on the scene with Their help.

Q. In February 2011, New Zealand was hit by a magnitude 6.3 earthquake, which devastated the central part of Christchurch city. Japan and New Zealand are in the same earthquake zone and have similar geographical conditions. Was there any connection between those two earthquakes? (April 2011)

A. Yes, there is major seismic activity taking place in the whole Pacific ring. We should not be surprised by further earthquake and/or tsunami activity elsewhere in that area.

Q. Concerning the horrific earthquake and tsunami which has just taken place in Japan, can you say if it is karmic or comes from natural causes? (April 2011)

A. The Japanese earthquake and the recent one in New Zealand had natural causes, to do with the movements of the Pacific Plates in the so-called 'Ring of Fire' earthquake zone of the Pacific. If you read the Master's article 'Man's responsibility' [page 115], however, you will see that there is a karmic causation, stemming from humanity as a whole, acting in destructive ways. If humanity were less destructive, so too would be earthquake, volcanic and cyclonic activity.

THE EARTH IN TRAVAIL

by the Master —, through Benjamin Creme

It may be said that at last some men are beginning to take seriously the dangers posed by global warming and the consequent climate changes that this is bringing about. It is true that there is much disagreement over the reality and extent of the dangers, and of the best means of approaching the problems which are agreed to exist. However, there is no doubt that some men, at least, are recognising that men face a formidable task in halting the progress of destruction and in stabilising the environment. It is also true that even the most aware and concerned of men know little of the extent and complexity of the problems.

The problem of pollution is such a case. Pollution takes many forms, some obvious and easily dealt with, if the will to do so exists. Some, however, require a science and a remedy as yet unknown to man; they are so toxic and destructive that they must be given high priority to overcome. The effect of pollution on the quality of air, food, on animals, and on fish, in rivers and the oceans, is known but largely ignored. The most destructive of all, that caused by nuclear radiation, awaits discovery by Earth scientists. The upper levels of nuclear radiation are beyond the present atomic technology. They are also the most toxic and hazardous to man and the lower kingdoms. On all those levels the problems of pollution must be overcome. This can be achieved only by a complete reconstruction of the present political, economic and social structures.

Man has ravaged and polluted the Earth, and severely damaged his own environment. Now man must see it as a top priority to remedy what he has hurt and so restore to health his ailing planet. He must learn to simplify his demands on the planet and learn the beauty of simplicity and the joy of sharing.

Man has but little choice: the urgency of the task demands immediate action; few indeed realise the true scale of damage already done. The question may be asked: can planet Earth be saved and by what means?

The answer is a resounding YES! and by means which involve the transformation of the present modes of living by the majority of men.

The paramount ambition of all so-called 'developed' countries is to achieve an ever higher percentage of growth of their economies to become, thereby, richer; and, in an economic world based on competition, to attain dominance and power, and so enjoy a higher standard of life. This being so, the pillaging of the Earth, the cavalier waste of resources, is seen as only natural and necessary. This irresponsible action has at last brought planet Earth almost to its knees.

Maitreya, you can be sure, will not be long in addressing this urgent problem and in presenting His solutions. The first step, He will advocate, is the acceptance of the urgency which many today deny. Sharing, He will say, is the beginning of the process of change which will provide the answers to our woes and the rehabilitation of Earth.

(*Share International*, November 2007)

NUCLEAR RADIATION AND
NUCLEAR POWER PLANTS

Q. (1) What is the best way to convince medical science that, whether or not nuclear plants have accidents, suffer disasters, leaks, and so on, the very fact that they exist at all is dangerous and highly toxic? (2) Would further developments in Kirlian photography technology provide effective proof? (3) If not, which scientific approach would lead most rapidly to finding proof of how polluting nuclear energy is? (July/August 2011)

A. (1) If it were possible I would have done so long ago. I have been speaking about the dangers of nuclear radiation for 30 years or more. These 'scientists' will listen only to their own kind, who unfortunately share the same set of blinkers. (2) No. (3) The experience of disasters like the ones at Fukushima, Chernobyl, etc.

Q. Hierarchical advice is that all nuclear plants should be closed as soon as possible. (1) Scientists say that nuclear energy is cleaner than carbon-based energy. (2) There are no really efficient alternatives. (3) So much money is invested in the nuclear industry it is virtually impossible to extricate our economies from it. Could you please comment on the issues raised above? (July/August 2011)

A. (1) In terms of carbon yes, but not in terms of destructiveness. (2) The alternative is the fusion process of nuclear energy. It does not depend on fission. It is clean, cold, does not provide waste and according to the Master Djwhal Khul (Who gave the Alice A. Bailey teachings) requires only a simple isotope of water, available worldwide, in order to satisfy our need for power. There are various formulae for the fusion process, some of which have already been bought up by branches of the oil industry to protect their domain. (3) This is true of the more sophisticated industrial nations but not for the whole world. We do not need power stations based on nuclear fission. They are out of date and extremely dangerous.

Q. *Could your Master please say how the world's energy needs can be met in the short to medium term, supposing that the world follows Hierarchy's advice to stop using nuclear energy.* (July/August 2011)

A. The cold fusion process (see above question).

Q. *Is the complete cessation of all activities involving nuclear energy produced by fission likely to take place within the next 25 years?* (July/August 2011)

A. Yes.

Q. *A certain amount of nuclear energy is needed for medical applications. Does the world also need to phase that out? What would replace it in the short term?* (July/August 2011)

A. This will be superseded by the coming advanced form of genetic engineering.

Q. *Since Fukushima, a so-called "nuclear stress test" has been developed. (1) Do you think it is rigorous enough? (2) Is the stress test an honest, un-manipulated attempt to prove safety and highlight dangers?* (July/August 2011)

A. (1) No. (2) It may be an honest attempt but it is certainly not an effective one. The whole point is that the technology of nuclear science today is inadequate to measure the whole range of the energy of matter.

Q. *Is a significant drop in the current standard of living and comfort an inevitable outcome of getting rid of atomic energy?* (July/August 2011)

A. No, by no means.

Q. Where are the most dangerous nuclear plants at present around the globe? (July/August 2011)

A. All plants that are more than 20 years old are particularly suspect whether they have had an accident or not.

Q. Is genetic disruption and mutation an unavoidable consequence of exposure to nuclear pollution? (July/August 2011)

A. Yes.

Q. Germany has announced it will abandon nuclear energy in the coming years. Do you think other countries will follow suit? (July/August 2011)

A. Yes, in time.

Q. Tokyo Electric Power company and various experts are still debating about what to do with the damaged nuclear power plants in Fukushima, Japan. In the meantime, the Japanese government has been telling the evacuees who used to live in the surrounding towns and villages that they are working hard to enable them to return to their homes as soon as possible. I think the government is giving them false hope when you think of the Chernobyl situation where the surrounding areas are still off limits 25 years after the power plant accident. Will you please comment on this situation? (March 2012)

A. It is not the same kind of reactor as that of Chernobyl, and the situation is therefore not the same. It is too early to say with any degree of confidence whether it can be restored or whether it needs to be abandoned completely. The situation is changing all the time and is not stable. With tremendous good luck and the hard work of the engineers, it is possible that it could be restored and that the people could return in a few years or longer. My Master advises extreme caution in considering returning to live there.

Q. In which parts of the world were or are the levels of radiation due to the catastrophe in Japan of last month critical? (May 2011)

A. Nowhere. There has been an extraordinarily hysterical reaction to the Japanese power plant accident. So far, the only people affected by radiation are those living in the north-eastern part of Japan.

Q. Had we better stop eating fish as all the seas are connected?(May 2011)

A. All the oceans and land masses of the world are already affected to some extent with nuclear radiation, as too is the air we breathe. The Space Brothers spend 90 per cent of Their time and effort in neutralising it (within Karmic Law). We wantonly deplete fish stocks worldwide but, to put things in perspective, there are still a lot of fish in the sea.

THE WAY MAITREYA WORKS

Q. Why does Maitreya think that it is necessary for Him to physically emerge in order to complete the shift in human consciousness? (October 2007)

A. Maitreya has physically returned to the everyday world as part of the similar return that the Hierarchy of Masters are undergoing. It is called the Externalisation of the Hierarchy. Over and above that, He has returned in a full, physical sense so that He can do His work as the World Teacher for the Aquarian Age. Were He not in a physical form, He would not gain the attention of countless millions who require someone they can see and hear directly. Even now, many who would gladly believe He is here, and are ready to respond to His Teaching, are hesitant because they cannot see Him. Countless others, in the meantime, chase after gurus and dubious avatars, because they have to see a physical person to relate to.

Q. Can Maitreya's physical body contain all the consciousness of the energy of Christ, or just a small percentage of it? (April 2008)

A. Not just a small percentage of it but yes, it does contain 85 per cent.

Q. Is Maitreya a channel for the energy of Christ, or is his physical body different from ours? (April 2008)

A. Maitreya is so pure and so advanced that He does not simply channel the Christ consciousness but Embodies it completely. It flows directly from Him to us. His 'Body of Light' is 'at rest' in the Himalayas. The body in which He manifests today is created by Himself.

Q. What reaction does Maitreya have towards the right-wing evangelicals in the United States? They seem extreme and dangerous to me. (June 2009)

A. I have no doubt whatsoever that He loves them as He loves you: totally and unconditionally.

Q. When it comes to helping Maitreya to fulfil his mission, which would include all religions, what about those that have a guru? When someone is following another Master or Guru how can this be combined? (March 2009)

A. Maitreya is not a religious teacher. He is essentially a Spiritual Teacher including a concern about the political, economic and social needs of the world. He is the World Teacher for all people, religious or not. Most people tend to see the religious path as the only spiritual path. It is only one of many paths to the experience of God. We have so enshrouded politics and economics in a deep materialism that we have landed ourselves in the critical conditions of today. We must have spiritual politics and economics through sharing, justice and freedom for all people. That is the aim of Maitreya. Love is the action of just sharing. That is the way to peace. No one need even believe in the reality of Maitreya. It is enough to believe in what He stands for. He does not want followers or devotees.

Q. A year and a half ago Maitreya began His open mission (television interview in the US and other countries). Since then we have had the Gulf oil disaster, the Japanese tsunami and its continuing radioactive fallout, the Arab Spring with many getting killed or beaten horrifically, and freak weather patterns continuing to cause havoc around the world. I had hoped that Maitreya's presence and influence would take us in a more benevolent and peaceful direction. It appears that is not the case and that His presence does not mean less upheaval. In fact, there may be more of the same and worse until a turning point is reached. Can you comment on this seeming dichotomy and at what point might we expect that turning point? Thank you for all your good work over the years. (November 2011)

A. Naturally, given the difference between their point of evolution and experience, ordinary people and the Masters see the happenings of the world in completely different ways. We see only a sequence of isolated events and, depending on our state of mind, often see them only as threatening, unwelcome or terrifying. The Masters see the same events but also all the other events that are happening simultaneously on all planes, which we do not see because of our limited awareness. The Masters see events rising and descending through the planes. Many of the events which to us are so powerful and threatening, to the Masters' vision wither away and disappear, while at the same time great energetic movements embodying new structures, thoughts and ideas gradually descend and manifest on the physical plane. In this way a tremendous transformation is taking place of which, for the most part, humanity has no knowledge.

The questioner asks when we can expect the turning point in this process. The turning point has already begun. More and more of the 'new' is becoming concrete on the lower planes, less and less of the 'garbage' of the past is now asserting its influence. Relatively very soon we shall become aware of a 'calming' of the world and as humanity acts – it all depends on humanity's action – so the leavening of the new can take place. Humanity has to see itself as a force in action, not simply as hopeful onlookers to these tremendous events. As Maitreya says: "Nothing happens by itself. Man must act and implement his will." This, humanity is beginning to do.

Q. This is a question about diversity in presenting the Reappearance story. If it is true that four other senior disciples refused to present it to the public, then perhaps the story has so far been presented from one perspective only, that is, as a continuation of the Blavatsky/Bailey work. Would you like to comment, please? (March 2007)

A. True indeed, it has been, but I have never said these four others were senior disciples. I said there were four other disciples. There is a difference. None of them were in touch with a Master. If they had been, they would probably have acted as I have. If I had not been in touch with a Master and had received the information as they probably received it, I may not have acted either. But I had a Master saying: "Go on, get out and tell it to the world."

It was not my idea at all to go out and talk to the world. I would never have done it had I not been rather pushed to do it! So I do not blame those others for not coming forward. It is true, therefore, that it has largely come through as a continuation of the Blavatsky/Alice Bailey information, which is I believe the correct one. I could never have presented it in any other way. I am steeped in the Blavatsky and Alice Bailey teachings, which I believe are the direct teachings from Hierarchy. I am only interested in what I believe to be the truth.

Nevertheless, there are other ways in which this information could be presented. You could be a believing Christian. I am sure many people in the groups are believing Christians. They could go out and talk about this as the return of the Christ, and would not need to refer to Alice Bailey or Blavatsky or any of the teaching given. It could be presented in many different ways. I am not these other people, so I cannot present it in any other way than I do. But I am absolutely certain it can be presented in other ways.

For example, Muslims await the Imam Mahdi. There were two Pakistani men who were sent to London about the time when Maitreya came there. They both had met a 'holy man', one in Lahore and the other in Karachi. They did not know each other and the holy men were different but each told them the same story – that they were to go to London to prepare the way for the Imam Mahdi. One man was a journalist and involved in politics. He said: "No, I cannot. I have my work. I am a journalist and I am a member of the political party of Benazir Bhutto's father" (before Bhutto was killed). He said: "There is no way I can go." The holy man had told him months earlier that he would have to go to London, and had given him things he had lost years before and knew things about his family that only his family knew. The holy man presented himself as somebody who was very knowledgeable. He said: "If you do not go, events will conspire to force you to go."

The same thing happened with the other man, who was a lawyer. He said: "I cannot go. I have my law practice." The holy man said: "If you do not go, events will conspire to force you to go."

The upshot was that Mr Bhutto was killed and anybody connected with him became suspect. They were looking for members of Bhutto's party. I do not know what position the journalist held, but he was well-connected in the party. He had a brother living in the Asian community of London. He gave up his job and went to London, and got work as a journalist on a Pakistani paper.

The lawyer, meanwhile, found his business failing, and before it got too low he just sold it for the goodwill of his practice and he too went off to London. Those two men did not know each other, and did not meet until I put a full-page advertisement in one of the newspapers in the Asian community in London, saying that the Mahdi had returned to the world and was living in the Asian community in London. The information went around the community. These two men from Pakistan read it. It so happened that the brother of one knew the other. So he invited the two together, and they found out that they had had exactly the same experience. Each in different cities, different holy men had given them exactly the same instruction. So they decided to get in touch with me and I met them.

I had announced in May 1982 that Maitreya was in the Asian community of London, and that if well-known journalists of calibre went through the motions of looking for Him, He would come forward to them. I expected many foreign journalists to do this and asked these men to act as their guides into that rather closed Asian community, and they agreed.

However, the one who was a journalist just waited for Maitreya to tap him on the shoulder. The other read all he could about the Imam Mahdi, and in the process he turned himself into a devout Muslim. Since then he has written a book about the coming to the world of the Imam Mahdi.

You can present this information in the way of Christians, of Muslims, of Buddhists. Maitreya Buddha is awaited by all Buddhists. Japanese Buddhists think it is still about 5 billion 670 million years ahead, so there is no hurry. It can be presented as being about Krishna or Kalki Avatar, or as the Jewish Messiah. These all refer to Maitreya, whether knowingly or not.

I present it in the Hierarchical way, which I believe to be the most informed, the most true, the most profound, the least distorted. All the religious ways are distorted to some degree. It has taken hundreds or thousands of years for them to come down to us, and they all get distorted. Every holy scripture is discoloured to some degree. Only in the esoteric teaching, I believe, do you receive the correct information.

If you are in touch with a Master, that is the best of all. You do not need any books or any other teaching. You can speak directly and that is the best. But that is rare; that is really rather rare.

Q. There is a tendency in people to deliberately harm other living creatures, such as the tormenting and torturing of fellow men and animals, and to derive 'satisfaction' from that. Does this stem from a helpless suffering from imperfection, incompleteness, separateness? It seems to me that this cannot be found in animals. (January/February 2006)

A. From imperfection, separateness and complacency. From a non-understanding of the Law of Cause and Effect or Karma, the Law of Rebirth and the Law of Harmlessness. There is, also, worldwide, pent up anger and frustration passed on from generation to generation by conditioning, which erupts in people and is vented in the appalling cruelty described.

Q. (1) I have heard of people in near death situations being saved through some kind of divine intervention. Why do some people receive these miracles but not others? It seems God is being unfair here. (2) Maitreya likes to call us "complacent". This is judgemental. I thought He would be against judgement. (May 2006)

A. (1) This is regulated by the Law of Cause and Effect or Karma. People are helped or cured according to their karmic condition. Our actions in this and previous lives – whether harmless or destructive – determine what happens. (2) I do not know if Maitreya 'likes' to call us complacent. The fact is we in the West *are* complacent in the face of so much hunger and unnecessary suffering in the world. It is one of the chief factors in our ability to accept such cruelty.

Q. What will Maitreya bring that is markedly different from the truths that have been spoken over previous generations? (October 2008)

A. His love, His wisdom, His mind, His energy. There has never been an Avatar better equipped than Maitreya is today.

Q. What is the difference between true and false hope? (November 2009)

A. True hope emanates from the soul and is therefore a spiritual quality. It fills the person with the desire to seek and visualise an aspiration for future betterment and is therefore a driving force for evolution itself. That is why, for humanity, hope is an essential aspect of life.

False hope, on the other hand, is the expression of an emotional desire for belief, help and security. It is essentially the outcome of fear and frequently leads to disappointment.

Q. Free will is sacrosanct. However, are there limits to that free will? As an example, what if someone was going to kill him or herself? The police would be called and the individual would be stopped. Would people be obligated to intervene under such circumstances or is free will sacrosanct under any and all circumstances, as long as others are not harmed? Should people be allowed to do what they want as long as it doesn't hurt someone else? (July/August 2011)

A. Humanity's free will, seen from the point of view of the Masters, is sacrosanct and They do not infringe it. That limits the degree to which the Masters can help humanity. That is the Law. Humanity itself has a limited free will, depending on the person's level of evolution. The more evolved, the more that person will act within the Law and so

138

have free will. The less evolved a person is, the less he or she lives within the Law of Cause and Effect – karma – and so has less control over it.

Q. I have a question about 'spiritual tension', which is mentioned in some of your books: What is it exactly? How can I achieve it? You describe 'winding up the tension' but I'm unclear about what it is. (December 2011)

A. Spiritual tension results, for some, from a focus on and identification with a spiritual ideal, or, for others, the practice of Maitreya's precepts – honesty of mind, sincerity of spirit and detachment. Focusing the mind in this way serves to 'wind up' the tension.

Q. Is there something of a natural masculine and feminine 'essence', a different quality that can be expressed or experienced by men and women only (or dominantly), and which are not the physical-biological differences nor what is inherited by culture? (December 2011)

A. Yes. This is a reflection of the spiritual reality of Father/Mother God.

HUMANITY'S CHOICE

HUMANITY'S CHOICE AND THE SPEED OF CHANGE

This article is an edited answer that Benjamin Creme gave at the Transmission Meditation Conference in San Francisco, USA, in August 2001 (before the events of 9/11).

Everyone in the world has the responsibility for maintaining the peace of the world. Practically, in the so-called democracies, people who have some sort of say – even if it is only by putting their vote down on a card in a system that may or may not be fair and incorrupt – have the responsibility of using their voice and bringing a result in that way. They perhaps have more responsibility than the starving millions of the world, the poor, the hungry, those who have no connection to any political structure whatsoever and so have no means of making their needs felt.

Needless to say, they have the greatest needs of all but no voice. It is precisely that voice which Maitreya will give to them. He will give voice to the needs of the poor, the hungry, the displaced, and those sitting in jail throughout the world. Hundreds of thousands of people are in jail simply for the crime of having a different point of view from their present government. It is taken for granted that they be incarcerated and languish in prison, very often tortured to boot. They have no voice. Maitreya will speak for them and for all who need a voice but have none.

Those who have a voice, education, a voting system, and a degree of democracy have a special responsibility. It is the responsibility of the American people, for example, to change the views of your president in so far as they affect the world as a whole. Where they affect only America his voice is probably as important as yours. But where they affect the world as a whole, he has only a tiny voice among all the voices in the world. You must reduce that tiny voice to accommodate the views of the rest of the world.

America is rich (whether it will maintain that wealth or not remains to be seen), militarily powerful, and the only superpower today. These facts have gone to the head of the US President [George W. Bush]. He has become hysterical in his use of that power. He wants to establish America as not only safe but impregnable to all comers. It is impossible today to make any single country impregnable, not even a country as large as the United States, not even as large as the Soviet Union used to be, which covered one-sixth of the world. You see how impregnable they were? Likewise, nothing stands still. Nothing remains the same for ever. The United States of America is no more the end product of a blueprint today than the Soviet Union was an end product of the blueprint that established it in 1917.

Things move and change. It is up to you, the people of the United States, to see that your President changes his views. He has up to now refused to sign the Kyoto Agreement. He is not alone in this, but almost alone among the great powers: 180 other nations have signed that agreement and will insist on its ratification and implementation.

When Maitreya comes out I think you will find there will be two responses: a welcoming response, and a response of the fundamentalists of all kinds, not just Christians, who will look at this with great concern. Some, a minority, will think this is the Antichrist. And they will be believed by a relatively small number, a minority of fundamentalist Christians. The fundamentalist Jews are waiting for the Messiah. They are going to find it quite difficult to accept Maitreya as the Messiah. But when they do, it will transform the entire scene in the Middle East.

I am talking about the political effects of this, the gaining of unity through political action. This is what the latter part of the Master's article on 'Unity' was largely about: the dangers to the world and the need for the realisation by all people, particularly the educated, authoritative and articulate people of the world to make known, to see, to understand the need for unity on an international scale. Hence the necessity for all the nations to work together. Nothing will change unless this occurs.

Transformation

Many people imagine that Maitreya is going to come out and start speaking, and the Masters one by one will be brought forward and start speaking, and the world will listen to Them and start changing. It is not as simple as that. Everything has to be done by humanity. That means any change has to have, not necessarily 100 per cent consensus, but a large degree of approval by most of the people in the world. Otherwise the change will not stick. It would be an infringement of free will if humanity made decisions on the strength of advice from Maitreya or any of the Masters, which had not already had the approval of the vast majority of humanity.

We are no longer going to go on a simple majority like a political party. But that reality, the reality of decision-making by the majority, will persist, to a degree, for a long time, aided by the advice of the Masters, which will help to form it and transform it into a consensus. But unless there is a degree of consensus nothing will happen. There will be no changes. Anything imposed will not last unless it has the approval of the majority of the people.

Everything that is changed is open to counter-change. Everything that you make is open to its opposite. People will reflect: "Is this the best way to do this after all?" And they will come up with something else. It is a living, creative process. It is not just changing one set of structures for another. It is changing the present set of values for another set of values. These values are not held at the same level, with the same intensity by all the people. They are not lived by the masses who may think that they hold them.

The human psyche and its body of beliefs, expectations and hopes is a very complicated thing. But speaking broadly, humanity will be invited to put into practice that which at any given time has the greatest consensus. If it is 90 per cent of humanity who agree to a given change, I think that would be sufficient. But if it is only 50 per cent or even just a majority of 55 or 60 per cent of the majority for a given political or economic change, it will not be put into effect. The advice would be that it is not ready to be implemented because it would not last.

There are powerful forces in the world who see things in different ways. It has always been like that, and that habit of seeing things in a particular way has become institutionalised. The habit, the conditioning, is so strong, the glamour goes so deep, that humanity as a whole is going to take a long time, and with much heart-searching, to find consensus. So you should not look for dramatic changes in the immediate future. The changes will take place gradually with the minimum of upset, the minimum of destruction or conflict in the societies of the world. Whatever is acceptable will be implemented. Where it is not acceptable it will be held over until it is acceptable. It will only be acceptable when trust is created.

Trust

That trust will be created by economic change. The starting point of the answer to all our problems is the economic redistribution of the world's resources. That is the key to all further changes because it creates trust. When you create trust all things become possible. Then you get changes in the political field, which make changes in the economic field easier. These changes make changes easier in the purely practical field of looking after the planet. Then not only America but the Europeans, Japan and some of the more powerful industrialised nations will have to look very seriously at their plans for implementing their agreements like the Kyoto Agreement, but also further agreements that will be brought forward and signed by large numbers of nations.

In this situation the United Nations will become the key factor. It will come into its own. Unfortunately today the United Nations as an institution is deeply frowned on by the more right-wing groups in the United States. It is a saving grace that the United Nations headquarters is actually in New York. If it were in London, Geneva, Darjeeling or Tokyo, a large section of the United States would have nothing to do with it. The US would not pay its dues. They would be very obstructive to everything the United Nations would want to do. And yet the developing world owes the United Nations a tremendous debt. It is one of the greatest educators of the world. It is one of the greatest providers of healthcare for millions of people who have no other means of healthcare. Without the United Nations, which is a triumph of modern society, millions of people would go wanting even more than they do. So you must give the United Nations every ounce of your strength and support.

In an Agni Yoga book introduced by Helena Roerich, Maitreya said: "There was a time when 10 true men could save the world. Then came a time when 10,000 was not enough. I shall call on 1 billion." There are 6 billion people in incarnation at the moment. Two or three years ago I asked my Master: "Has Maitreya actually got the billion?" He said: "A billion and a half." That has increased since then. It is now over 1.5 billion people [1.8 billion as of 2006] ready to respond to Maitreya, ready when He gives the word to come forward, to give their talents, their goodwill, to help in every way.

Restoration of the planet

Maitreya will set up pioneer corps that will go around the world implementing and administering the changes, first of all in the economic and political fields. When these changes are somewhat implemented, the restoration of the planet to health will be next. As my Master has said many times, and as Maitreya said in His messages (See *Messages from Maitreya the Christ*), this will be the number one

145

priority in the world. This is the bed in which we lie. This planet Earth is the source of our being, yet we are destroying it with every day that passes. The Master says that pollution is the number one killer in the world today. The world is being made deficient in resources. We are ruining the fabric of our world in so many ways. So it will become the number one work for all people – every man, every woman, and every child – to save the planet. Children are marvellous. When you set a child of about seven to 15 years of age the work of saving the planet, they will do it better than anyone else, not on the high scientific levels, but on the immediate level. They will make their mothers and fathers make a sustainable economy because unless we have a sustainable economy we will not have any economy at all. If it is not sustainable, the world has maybe another 15 years of life to give that we can stand, and then it will deteriorate very rapidly.

We have about 15 to 20 years [now in 2012 it is 10 to 15 years] to restore the world to health, which we can do with the recommendations of the Masters, certain tools the Masters will make available to help the process, and with the help of our Space Brothers in the cleaning up of our planet, especially the air. The very air we breathe is badly polluted today, above all with nuclear radiation, which we do not even recognise as a major polluting factor. It is the most dangerous pollutant to our immune system, and has a life that can go on for thousands of years. Our oceans, rivers, lakes, and streams, the Earth itself, are also polluted to an extreme degree and have to be cleaned up, and are being cleaned up in an ongoing way, within karmic limits, by our Space Brothers.

Activities of UFOs

When Maitreya makes Himself known, He will answer questions on a wide variety of subjects. One of them will be to do with the UFO phenomenon. The intense activity of the UFOs is mainly one of salvation of the Earth, but they also have been concerned for many years in creating what they call a platform for the World Teacher, a platform of unification and an energetic platform. It is a platform of unification and form. They have been engaged in creating an energetic network throughout the world. The so-called crop circles are an outer expression of the grid of energy they are making. They are replicating on the physical plane the network of magnetic energy that surrounds this planet. This energetic network on the physical plane will be part of a new type of energy that will be eventually introduced to the world. So the crop circles are not just to say: "We are here." We certainly know that, but also to say: "We are here for a certain purpose."

Maitreya will answer questions about the reality of the Space Brothers. But those who expect fleets of spaceships to come down and land in Times Square or Piccadilly Circus will wait a long time. As I have said many times, they are etheric physical, not dense physical. The dense physical aspect they have when seen is a temporary one. They simply lower their vibrational rate until they are seen, but they can raise it again until they disappear. So do not expect hundreds of thousands of simultaneous landings, the introduction by Maitreya of the head of the Venusian fleet to the American fleet and so on. It is not going to be like that.

UNITY

by the Master —, through Benjamin Creme

Whenever men meet together in large groups they adopt a different view of themselves and look at each other in a new way. They are emboldened, strengthened in their desire and gravitate to those who support their viewpoint. This may seem natural but why should it be so?

Essentially, all men inwardly seek unity and find its reflection in conformity of thought and ideas. This instinct is behind the formation of political parties and other groups. The ideological consensus acts as a magnet and strengthens the potency of the whole.

Groups and parties founder when the inner unity is disturbed. Unity is a soul quality and essential for the cohesion of the group. Too great an emphasis on individuals and personality differences thus tends to weaken the unifying ties which hold the group together.

This principle can be seen at work in every branch of human activity. The rise and fall of parties, groups and even of nations are conditioned by this law. Unity is strength, say men, and thus it is, for it is man's essential nature.

Unity is not too difficult to attain in the earlier stages of formation of a group; if the purpose of its inception is magnetic enough, that alone can hold the group together. However, time brings differences and discontent. Strong and varied voices arise and seek to impose their will. If the desire for unity is lost the group, at once, is threatened.

The underlying purpose of all life is the creation of unity, thus expressing the interconnectedness of all atoms. For most men, cosmos is a collection of separate material bodies, infinitely large and distant, inertly obeying mechanical laws of matter. In reality, cosmos, Space Itself, is a living entity, the Source of our Being, our Mother and Father. As souls, we know this to be so, and seek to give expression to the fundamental unity of our nature. A group, therefore, loses this unity at its peril. Without such unity it functions not as a group but blindly, without purpose and cohesion, a disparate collection of attitudes and conditioning.

We are entering the Age of the Group; Aquarius, and its energies, can be lived and experienced only in group formation. The major quality of Aquarius, too, is Synthesis. Its fusing and blending rays will impose themselves on the lives of all until, gradually, the higher alchemy achieves its beneficent purpose and the race of men are One. Thus will it be. Thus will men know the truth that Unity is strength, the essential nature of our Being, the purpose to which all men strive and to which all activities of men seek to give expression.

When Maitreya, Himself, emerges in the very near future, He will underline the need for unity in all our undertakings. He will show how essential it is that we find an identity of purpose, as men and as nations, in solving human problems, thus putting our potent individualities at the service of the group.

(*Share International*, July/August 2001)

THE 'HAND' OF MAITREYA

This photograph shows an extraordinary miracle: the handprint of Maitreya Himself, miraculously manifested on a bathroom mirror in Barcelona, Spain. It is not a simple handprint but a three-dimensional image with photographic detail.

First published in *Share International* magazine (October 2001), the 'Hand' is a means of invoking the healing energies and help of Maitreya. By placing your hand over the photograph or simply looking at it, Maitreya's healing and help can be manifested (subject to Karmic Law). Until Maitreya emerges fully, and we see His face, it is the closest He can come to us.

"My help is yours to command, you have only to ask."

— Maitreya, the World Teacher

from Message No. 49

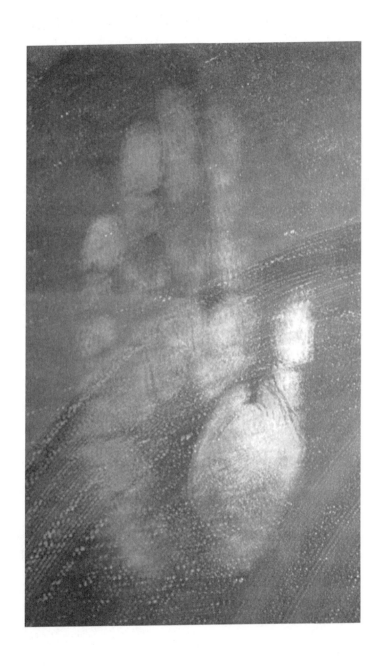

THE GREAT INVOCATION

From the point of Light within the Mind of God
Let light stream forth into the minds of men.
Let Light descend on Earth.

From the point of Love within the Heart of God
Let love stream forth into the hearts of men.
May Christ return to Earth.

From the centre where the Will of God is known
Let purpose guide the little wills of men –
The purpose which the Masters know and serve.

From the centre which we call the race of men
Let the Plan of Love and Light work out
And may it seal the door where evil dwells.

Let Light and Love and Power restore the Plan on Earth.

The Great Invocation, used by the Christ for the first time in June 1945, was released by Him to humanity to enable us to invoke the energies which would change our world and make possible the return of the Christ and Hierarchy. This World Prayer, translated into many languages, is not sponsored by any group or sect. It is used daily by men and women of goodwill who wish to bring about right human relations among all humanity.

THE PRAYER FOR THE NEW AGE

I am the creator of the universe.

I am the father and mother of the universe.

Everything comes from me.

Everything shall return to me.

Mind, spirit and body are my temples,

For the Self to realise in them

My supreme Being and Becoming.

The Prayer for the New Age, given by Maitreya, the World Teacher, is a great mantram or affirmation with an invocative effect. It will be a powerful tool in the recognition by us that man and God are One, that there is no separation. The 'I' is the Divine Principle behind all creation. The Self emanates from, and is identical to, the Divine Principle.

The most effective way to use this mantram is to say or think the words with focused will, while holding the attention at the ajna centre between the eyebrows. When the mind grasps the meaning of the concepts, and simultaneously the will is brought to bear, those concepts will be activated and the mantram will work. If it is said seriously every day, there will grow inside you a realisation of your true Self.

(First published in *Share International*, September 1988.)

TRANSMISSION MEDITATION

A brief explanation

A group meditation providing both a dynamic service to the world and powerful, personal spiritual development.

Transmission Meditation is a group meditation established to better distribute spiritual energies from their Custodians, the Masters of Wisdom, our planetary Spiritual Hierarchy. It is a means of 'stepping down' (transforming) these energies so that they become accessible and useful to the general public. It is the creation, in co-operation with the Hierarchy of Masters, of a vortex or pool of higher energy for the benefit of humanity.

In March 1974, under the direction of his Master, Benjamin Creme formed the first Transmission Meditation group in London. Today there are hundreds of Transmission Meditation groups around the world and new groups are forming all the time.

Transmission Meditation groups provide a link whereby Hierarchy can respond to world need. The prime motive of this work is service, but it also constitutes a powerful mode of personal growth. Many people are searching for ways in which to improve the world. This desire to serve can be strong, but difficult, in our busy lives, to fulfil. Our soul needs a means to serve, but we do not always respond to its call, and so produce disequilibrium and conflict within ourselves. Transmission Meditation provides a unique opportunity for service in a potent and fully scientific way with the minimum expenditure of one's time and energy.

Benjamin Creme holds Transmission Meditation workshops around the world. During the meditation he is overshadowed by Maitreya, the World Teacher, which allows Maitreya to confer great spiritual nourishment on the participants. Many people are inspired to begin Transmission Meditation after attending such a workshop, and many acknowledge having received healing in the process.

[See Benjamin Creme, *Transmission: A Meditation for the New Age,* Share International Foundation.]

BOOKS BY BENJAMIN CREME

The Reappearance of the Christ and the Masters of Wisdom

This classic of esoteric literature was Benjamin Creme's first book and gives the background and pertinent information concerning the return of Maitreya, the World Teacher. Putting the most profound event of the last 2,000 years into its correct historical and esoteric context, Benjamin Creme describes the effect the World Teacher's presence will have on both the world's institutions and the average person. Topics range from the soul and reincarnation to nuclear energy, UFOs, and a new economic order.
1st edition 1979. 2nd edition 2007. ISBN: 978-90-71484-32-2, 288pp.

Messages from Maitreya the Christ

During the years of preparation for His emergence, Maitreya gave 140 messages through Benjamin Creme during public lectures, using mental overshadowing and the telepathic rapport thus set up. The messages inspire readers to spread the news of His reappearance and to work urgently for the rescue of millions suffering from poverty and starvation in a world of plenty. When read aloud, the messages invoke Maitreya's energy and blessing.
1st edition Vol. I 1981, Vol. II 1986. 2nd, combined, edition 1992, reprinted 2001. ISBN 978-90-71484-22-3, 286pp.

Transmission: A Meditation for the New Age

Describes a dynamic process, introduced to the world by Benjamin Creme's Master in 1974. Groups dedicated to world service transmit spiritual energies directed through them by the Masters of our Spiritual Hierarchy. While the prime motive of this work is service, it is also a powerful means of personal growth. Guidelines are given for the formation of Transmission Meditation groups, along with

answers to many questions relating to the work.
1st edition 1983. 5th edition 2006. ISBN 978-90-71484-35-3, 212pp.

A Master Speaks
Articles by Benjamin Creme's Master from the first 22 volumes of *Share International* magazine, designed to draw attention to the needs of the present and immediate future. Topics include reason and intuition, health and healing, the art of living, human rights, the end of hunger, sharing for peace, the rise of people power, life in the New Age, the role of man, and many more.
1st edition 1985. 3rd expanded edition 2004. ISBN 978-90-71484-29-2, 452pp.

Maitreya's Mission, Volume One
The first of a trilogy of books which further describe the emergence of Maitreya. This volume can be seen as a guidebook for humanity as it travels on its evolutionary journey. A wide range of subjects is covered, such as: the new teachings of Maitreya, meditation, karma, life after death, healing, social transformation, initiation, the role of service, and the Seven Rays.
1st edition 1986. 3rd edition 1993, reprinted 2010. ISBN 978-90-71484-08-7, 419pp.

Maitreya's Mission, Volume Two
This volume contains a diverse collection of Maitreya's teachings through His associate, His highly accurate forecasts of world events, descriptions of His miraculous personal appearances, and accounts of related phenomena and signs. It also includes unique interviews with Benjamin Creme's Master on current affairs. Future-related topics include new forms of government, schools without walls, energy and thought, the coming Technology of Light, and the art of Self-realisation.
1st edition 1993, reprinted 2004. ISBN 978-90-71484-11-7, 753pp.

The Ageless Wisdom Teaching

An overview of humanity's spiritual legacy, this book is a concise and easy-to-understand introduction to the Ageless Wisdom Teaching. It explains the basic tenets of esotericism, including: the source of the Teaching, the origin of man, the Plan of evolution, rebirth and reincarnation, and the Law of Cause and Effect (karma). Also included is an esoteric glossary and a recommended reading list.

1st edition 1996, reprinted 2009. ISBN 978-90-71484-13-1, 79pp.

Maitreya's Mission, Volume Three

Benjamin Creme presents a compelling vision of the future, with Maitreya and the Masters openly offering Their guidance and inspiration. Coming times will see peace established; sharing the world's resources the norm; maintaining our environment a top priority. Cities of the world will become centres of great beauty. Benjamin Creme also looks at ten famous artists – among them Leonardo da Vinci, Michelangelo and Rembrandt – from a spiritual perspective.

1st edition 1997. 2nd edition 2010. ISBN 978-90-71484-45-2, 694pp.

The Great Approach: New Light and Life for Humanity

Addresses the problems of our chaotic world and its gradual change under the influence of Maitreya and the Masters of Wisdom. It covers such topics as sharing, the USA's quandary, ethnic conflicts, crime, environment and pollution, genetic engineering, science and religion, education, health and healing. It predicts amazing scientific discoveries ahead and shows a world free of war where the needs of all are met.

Part One "Life Ahead for Humanity"; Part Two "The Great Approach"; Part Three "The Coming of a New Light".

1st edition 2001. ISBN 978-90-71484-23-0, 320pp.

The Art of Co-operation

Deals with the urgent problems of our time and their solution, based on the Ageless Wisdom Teaching. Locked in ancient competition, we are trying to solve problems using out-worn methods, while the answer – co-operation – lies within our grasp. The book points the way to a world of justice, freedom and peace through a growing appreciation of the unity underlying all life.

Part One "The Art of Co-operation"; Part Two "The Problem of Glamour"; Part Three "Unity".

1st edition 2002. ISBN 978-90-71484-26-1, 235pp.

Maitreya's Teachings: The Laws of Life

Presents the Laws of Life, Maitreya's direct, simple, non-doctrinal and profound insights. Demonstrating the Law of Karma, or Cause and Effect, these extraordinary forecasts of world events were given by Maitreya between 1988 and 1993 and first published in *Share International* magazine. Edited by Benjamin Creme.

Few could read from these pages without being changed. To some the extraordinary insights into world events will be of major interest, while to others the laying bare of the secrets of self-realization, the simple description of experienced truth, will be a revelation. To anyone seeking to understand the Laws of Life, these subtle and pregnant insights will take them quickly to the core of Life itself, and provide them with a simple path stretching to the mountain-top. The essential unity of all life is underscored in a clear and meaningful way. Never, it would appear, have the Laws by which we live seemed so natural and so unconstraining.

1st edition, 2005. ISBN 978-90-71484-31-5, 258pp.

The Art of Living: Living Within the Laws of Life

In Part One, Benjamin Creme describes the experience of living as a form of art, like painting or music. To reach a high level of expression requires knowledge and application of fundamental principles such as the Law of Cause and Effect and the Law of Rebirth, all described in detail. Parts

Two and Three explain how we can emerge from the fog of illusion to become whole and Self aware.

Part One "The Art of Living"; Part Two "The Pairs of Opposites"; Part Three "Illusion".

1st *edition 2006. ISBN 978- 90-71484-37-7, 215pp.*

The World Teacher for All Humanity

Presents an overview of the return to the everyday world of Maitreya and His group, the Masters of Wisdom; the enormous changes Maitreya's presence has already brought about; and His recommendations for the immediate future. It describes Maitreya as a great spiritual Avatar of immeasurable love, wisdom and power; and also as a friend and brother of humanity, here to lead us into the age of Aquarius.

1st edition, 2007. ISBN 978-90-71484-39-1, 132pp.

The Awakening of Humanity

A companion volume to *The World Teacher for All Humanity*, which emphasises the nature of Maitreya as the Embodiment of Love and Wisdom, while *The Awakening of Humanity* focuses on the day when Maitreya declares Himself openly as World Teacher for the age of Aquarius. It describes the process of Maitreya's emergence, the steps leading to the Day of Declaration, and humanity's anticipated response to this momentous event.

1st edition 2008. ISBN 978-90-71484-41-4, 141pp.

The Gathering of the Forces of Light: UFOs and Their Spiritual Mission

The Gathering of the Forces of Light is a book about UFOs, but with a difference. It is written by someone who has worked with them and knows about them from the inside. Benjamin Creme sees the presence of UFOs as planned and of immense value for the people of Earth.

According to Benjamin Creme, the UFOs and the people in them are engaged on a spiritual mission to ease humanity's lot and to save this planet from further and faster destruction. Our own planetary Hierarchy, led by Maitreya, the World Teacher, now living among us, works tirelessly with their Space Brothers in a fraternal enterprise to restore sanity to this Earth.

Topics covered in this unique book include: the Space Brothers' work on Earth; George Adamski; crop circles; the new Technology of Light; Benjamin Creme's work with the Space Brothers; the dangers of nuclear radiation; saving the planet; the 'star' heralding Maitreya's emergence; Maitreya's first interview; education in the New Age; intuition and creativity; family and karma.

Part One "UFOs and Their Spiritual Mission"; Part Two "Education in the New Age".

1st edition 2010. ISBN 978-90-71484-46-9, 240pp.

~ ~ ~

Benjamin Creme's books have been translated and published in Dutch, French, German, Japanese and Spanish by groups responding to this message. Some have also been published in Chinese, Croatian, Finnish, Greek, Hebrew, Italian, Portuguese, Romanian, Russian, Slovenian and Swedish. Further translations are planned. Books are available from local booksellers as well as online vendors.

See also 'Other Languages' on the site: **www.share-international.org/books**

SHARE INTERNATIONAL MAGAZINE
ISSN 0169-1341

A unique magazine featuring each month: up-to-date information about the emergence of Maitreya, the World Teacher; an article from a Master of Wisdom; expansions of the esoteric teachings; Benjamin Creme's answers to a wide variety of topical and esoteric questions; articles by and interviews with people at the forefront of progressive world change; news from UN agencies and reports of positive developments in the transformation of our world.

Share International brings together the two major directions of New Age thinking the political and the spiritual. It shows the synthesis underlying the political, social, economic and spiritual changes now occurring on a global scale, and seeks to stimulate practical action to rebuild our world along more just and compassionate lines.

Share International covers news, events and comments related to Maitreya's priorities: an adequate supply of the right food, housing and shelter for all, healthcare and education as universal rights, and the maintenance of ecological balance in the world.

Versions of *Share International* are available in Dutch, French, German, Japanese, Romanian, Slovenian and Spanish. For subscription information, contact the appropriate office below.

For North, Central and South America, Australia, New Zealand and the Philippines
Share International
PO Box 5668, Santa Monica CA 90409 USA

For the UK
Share International
PO Box 3677, London NW5 1RU, UK

For the rest of the world
Share International
PO Box 41877, 1009 DB Amsterdam, Holland

For more information:
www.share-international.org

ABOUT THE AUTHOR

Scottish-born artist, author and lecturer Benjamin Creme has for almost 40 years been preparing the world for the most extraordinary event in human history – the return of our spiritual mentors to the everyday world.

Benjamin Creme has appeared on television, radio and in documentary films worldwide, and lectures throughout Western and Eastern Europe, the USA, Japan, Australia, New Zealand, Canada and Mexico.

Trained and supervised over many years by his own Master, he began his public work in 1974. In 1982 he announced that the Lord Maitreya, the long-awaited World Teacher, was living in London, ready to present Himself openly when invited by the media to do so. This event is now imminent.

Benjamin Creme continues to carry out his task as messenger of this inspiring news. His books, sixteen at present, have been translated into many languages. He is also the editor of *Share International* magazine, which circulates in over 70 countries. He accepts no money for any of this work.

Benjamin Creme lives in London, is married, and has three children.